The Chinese Language Demystified

Also by James Y. Hung:

Finding Fat Lady's Shoe: A Memoir of Growing up in Hong Kong and Malaysia. (2013)

FOB in Paradise: A Memoir. (2014)

Silk Road on My Mind. (2015)

Practical Ophthalmology: A Concise Manual for the Non-Ophthalmologist. (2016)

Available through Amazon in paperback and Kindle e-book. E-book also available through Barnes & Noble.

Finding Fat Lady's Shoe

An intensely reflective tale of a family uprooted by war, cast adrift onto a sea of uncertainty.—Kirkus Review

Dr. James Hung's life story echoes others that will probably never be written, and offers a fascinating perspective on Hong Kong's recent past that deserves to be widely read. [4 stars out of 5]—South China Morning Post

FOB in Paradise

Hung has written an absorbing and witty book. Dramatic, nuanced vignettes and vivid descriptions of people and places create a rich tapestry that shows the medical profession at its best and worst.

—Kirkus Review

Silk Road on My Mind

Hung is an endearing mix of benevolence, wryness, and curiosity....there is an appealing Marco Polo-ishness to his project: a boundless wonder for a society unlike his own, not for its differences but for the infinitely recognizable humanity at its center.—Kirkus Review

Practical Ophthalmology

More specialists should create guides of this caliber for nonspecialists. An indispensable ophthalmological volume for any general practitioner's office.

—Kirkus Review

The Chinese Language Demystified

James Y. Hung, MD

The Chinese Language Demystified

ISBN: 0692924957
EAN: 978-0692924952 (James Y. Hung)

Contents

Introduction

When I was in Greece some years ago, I learned that if the Greeks don't understand something, they say, 'It's Chinese to me' (i.e., it's incomprehensible). The French, too, have the expression, 'C'est du chinoise', meaning, *It's Chinese.* I wouldn't be surprised if other countries had similar sayings about the baffling nature of the Chinese language.

Most scholars agree that Chinese is one of the most difficult languages to learn. Imagine that instead of just having to learn the alphabet, which in the case of the English language consists of 26 letters, you would have to know around 2,000 characters in order to be literate in Chinese!

It's such a difficult language that many graduate students in Chinese studies cannot read fluently even in their 4th or 5th year of studies. This is quite a contrast compared to graduate students in, say, Spanish or French studies, who would learn to read fluently in those languages early on in their studies. Many Chinese graduate students also don't fully understand Chinese movies, because there are so many homonyms in the spoken language. This book will show how homonyms can make life confusing when one doesn't understand the context.

Most people know that Chinese has many dialects. Even though people from different regions cannot understand each other in speech, they can communicate with each other in the written language. How is that possible? It's possible because in contrast to a phonetic language, the characters are actually symbols just like numbers. No matter what language we speak, when we see '5', we all know what it means, whether we call it 'five' in

English, 'cinco' in Spanish, 'elima' in Hawaiian and so on. In the same way, when a Chinese person sees a character, no matter which dialect he or she speaks, it has the same meaning. For example, my family name is written 熊. In Mandarin it is pronounced 'Xiong', in Cantonese it is 'Hung', and in my own Hakka dialect it is 'Yung'. Since I grew up in Hong Kong, which primarily uses Cantonese, it appears in my documents as 'Hung'.

You will learn in this book that Chinese is not one language, but actually seven, which have been called major dialects. Even within these major dialects, regional differences make them unintelligible to each other, and sometimes, in mountainous regions where travel is infrequent, one village won't understand the dialect of the next village.

Chinese scholars have long been aware that Chinese is a very difficult language to learn, and during the past century, especially since the country became a Republic in 1912, language reform has become an urgent priority for the Chinese government. Several language reforms have been considered over the years, and one that has been implemented with some success is the simplification of some characters. But this has created a new problem in that the simplified characters are only used in Mainland China, but not in Taiwan, Hong Kong or among many of the Chinese diaspora in Southeast Asia. This means that now, instead of only one writing system, there are two, further complicating the language, especially for non-native speakers who want to learn Chinese.

Presently, there are about 100 million students studying Chinese as a second language throughout the world, and they are almost entirely studying the simplified version. If any of these students travelled to Hong Kong or Taiwan and tried to read the local paper, menu, instructions or street names, they would quickly realize that their knowledge of the simplified character system doesn't help them much.

Most Chinese language students know that what they learn is standard Mandarin or Putonghua, but few of them are aware that it is really a sort of artificial language originally constructed for the use of the non-Chinese Mongol and later the Manchu rulers who ruled China for several centuries.

Alphabet systems are extremely versatile. By combining a few letters in an alphabet, almost any sound in any language can be represented. Some languages in Central Asia such as Uyghur, Uzbek, Kazakh and Kyrgyz have used as many as four totally different alphabet systems (Sogdian, Arabic, Latin and Cyrillic) to write their language at different times in history, depending on the political situation or other conditions. By contrast, transforming the Chinese language into written form is a complicated process, as it involves many different characters that often have no intuitive connection to the way they sound when spoken.

From the spoken to the written forms of Chinese, and from the past to the present, this book looks at some of the dynamic aspects of the language that continue to fascinate people the world around. For those of you who have no intention of learning Chinese, you will at least understand some of the complexities to how the Chinese language works, and why it's so difficult to learn. For those of you who intend to study Chinese, you will have an idea of what to expect and will hopefully feel encouraged to know that you are not alone in your frustrations, and that the beauty of the language will be your reward.

I hope you find this book educational as well as entertaining.

1

My Language Journey

It has long been observed that for a child to learn to speak, he or she must be exposed to language before a certain age. Our brains are hard-wired for language, but if we don't use the neural resources reserved for that purpose, that capacity would then be used for other purposes. That's why language is easy for a child, and gradually becomes more difficult as we age. After puberty, it would be extremely difficult for someone to speak another language without any accent unless the second language was similar to their mother tongue.

The French movie *The Wild Child* by Francois Truffaut dramatizes the story of Victor of Aveyron. In 1797, a boy estimated to be around twelve was found wandering in a forest near Saint Sernin sur Rance, Aveyron, France. He walked on all fours and was naked, and had apparently lived alone in the woods his entire childhood. The boy was given the name Victor and put in a home, but he ran away several times. Three years after his final escape, he emerged from the forest on his own.

Victor's lack of speech, the numerous scars on his body and his food preferences indicated that he had been in the wild the majority of his life. A local abbot and biology professor took him in and, with the help of a medical student named Jean Marc Gaspard Itard, took on the plan to fully civilize the wild boy, who was estimated to be around fifteen by this time. Victor was judged to be of normal intelligence, and his hearing was tested and also found to be normal. He received intensive tutoring, but he was ultimately unable to learn to speak, and the only two words he could say were *lait* (milk) and *oh Dieu* (oh God).

There have been other similar cases of feral children who, in spite of concentrated efforts, were never able to learn to speak after the critical period had passed.

In the area of language learning, I was fortunate to be exposed to many dialects and languages at an early age, enabling my brain to use the neurons designed for this purpose to learn how to distinguish the phonemes (distinct units of sound in a specified language) of the different languages.

Shortly after I was born in China, I was frequently in the care of a wet nurse. She talked to me attentively and often, and took me with her to visit her friends, who would also talk to me. I soon began talking. This exposure no doubt stimulated my neural resources for language at the earliest age.

In 1949, when I was three, as China was falling to the communists, our family fled to Hong Kong. We settled in Kau Wa Keng, a village at the northern end of the Kowloon Peninsula and the beginning of the New Territories. This village was founded by Hakka people two or three hundred years ago; they too were refugees from the north. They spoke a Hakka dialect that was noticeably different from ours. Our Meixian Hakka is considered the standard. In a short time, I was able to communicate with the villagers in their form of Hakka, while at home I would switch back to our Meixian Hakka.

Prior to the influx of the million plus refugees fleeing the communists from all parts of China, the residents of Hong Kong were mostly from around the Guangzhou (Canton) area and only Cantonese was spoken. The medium of instruction in Hong Kong schools at that time was Cantonese.

I was seven when I began first grade. Our teacher was excellent, someone who took her job seriously and tried to make learning interesting for us. There were about thirty students in my class, with less than half being local Hakka residents and the rest consisting of refugees from all parts of China. I was fortunate that by the time I began school, I was able to speak fluent Cantonese. For some who had just arrived and who were not Cantonese, there was the added challenge of learning Cantonese first. For them, it was essentially like learning another language.

One student I remember vividly was a shy girl from Sichuan. The Sichuan dialect is a branch of the Mandarin dialect, but to outsiders it is incomprehensible, with strange intonations. Some boys in class would make fun of her because she simply could not say some of the Cantonese tones. After a year, she was much better, but still had an obvious accent. By the time she finished the fourth grade, she was able to speak Cantonese like the rest of us. At age seven, the neural resources for languages made learning easy for her.

It was at this same time that I was exposed to other dialects from Hubei, Shandong, Hunan, Fujian, Wuhan, Chongqing, Shanghai and other areas I had never heard of. All of these dialects were unintelligible to each other. My young brain tried very hard to differentiate the unique sounds of these dialects. Most adult refugees would never learn to speak Cantonese without an accent, sometimes very heavy ones, even after having lived in Hong Kong for decades.

Learning Chinese was an intensive process involving rote memorization and repetition. We had lots of homework and had to practice writing the new characters in an exercise book with squares, so that a character fit into each square. After the first year, I had learnt enough characters to express myself in a diary. Certainly my vocabulary was very limited, but I knew enough characters to put my thoughts down. For characters that I didn't know, I would make a symbol, draw a picture or use a character of similar sound but different meaning to substitute. For example, if I didn't know how to write the character 狗 (*dog*), which is pronounced 'kau' in Cantonese, I would substitute the character 九 (*nine*), which also has the sound 'kau' but only has two strokes, whereas the word for *dog* has eight strokes. So when I read my diary, I would know that I had substituted a character; otherwise, the sentence wouldn't make any sense.

Our teacher told us that Chinese was the oldest written language in the world and that we should be proud of our heritage. (Sumerian was the oldest written language, but it was discontinued. Chinese is the oldest written language still in use.) She showed us a few examples of how some characters looked when they were invented about four thousand years ago and compared them to their present forms. The top row here shows the original pictographs; the characters below are the present forms:

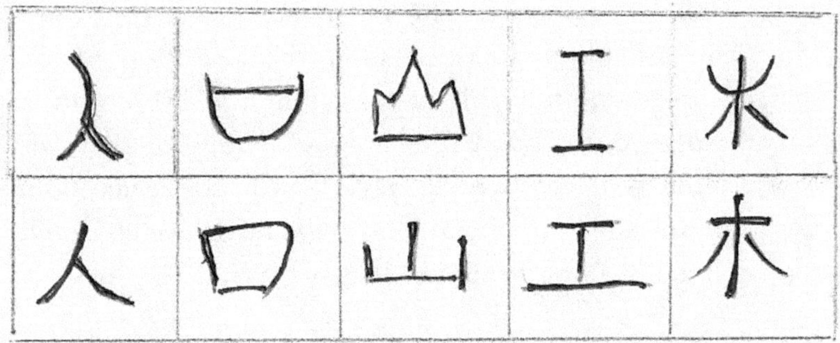

From left to right:

1. Man or person. This pictographic form represents a walking man.
2. Mouth.
3. Mountain. It clearly represents mountain peaks.
4. Work, labor. The pictographic form represents a carpenter's square.
5. Wood, tree.

We started learning the basic units called 'strokes', which are marks made with a single continuous motion of the pen. We learned about radicals, which are certain component parts of characters made up of strokes. We learned the three general categories of strokes, which were dots, lines and hooks. These strokes are the building units of Chinese characters. The radicals are then put together to form a character. Each character is one syllable and a word can be more than one character. Below are some examples of the radicals that make up a Chinese character.

One stroke: (—) horizontal; (I) vertical; (.) dot; (J) hook

王 玉 The first character is 'wang' or *king*. By adding a dot, it is 'yu' or *jade*.

Two strokes: 二 = two; 刀 = knife; 又 = also ; 人 = person

Three strokes: 口 = mouth; 土 = earth; 女 = woman; 山= mountain

Four strokes: 心 = heart; 手 = hand; 日 = sun; 月= moon

Five strokes: 玉 = jade; 生= live; 田= field; 石= stone

Six strokes: 竹 = bamboo; 米= rice; 耳= ear; 肉 = meat

Seven strokes: 見= see; 言= speech; 足= foot; 走 = run

Eight strokes: 金= gold; 長= long; 門= door; 青 = green

There are probably fewer than two hundred radicals. Some are used often and some are rarely used. Some have as many as fourteen or more strokes.

We learned to put radicals together to form characters. The following are two examples of such a process.

口 This is the radical 'mouth'.

木 This is the radical 'wood'.

By combining the two, with *wood* on top and *mouth* on the bottom, it becomes 杏, which reads 'xing' and means *apricot*.

The second example is made by using the same two radicals, but with *mouth* on top and *wood* at the bottom, so that it becomes 呆, which reads 'dai' and means *foolish*.

Modifications often have to be made so that the relative proportions of the individual strokes enable the whole character to fit into a square space. Note the radical 'mouth' in *apricot* looks different from the one in *foolish*.

We learned to write in the correct sequence of strokes, then to combine them to form characters. Each stroke has to be written correctly, in the proper sequence, and the rules dictate that we write the 'top before bottom' and 'left before right'.

We also learned early on to vary the size of the strokes so that the total effect would be balanced, and no matter how simple or complex the characters were, they would be written so that they take up the same amount of square space.

Our teacher showed us an extreme example of how we must learn to fit each character into one square, whether it consisted of one stroke or 64. The example she gave us is pronounced 'zhe' and means 'verbose'.

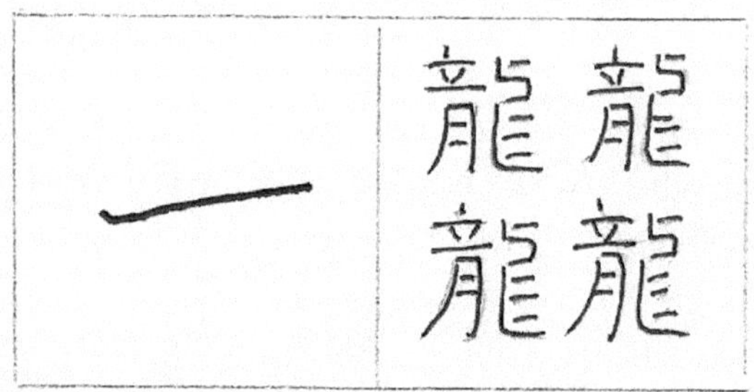

Earlier, I explained how the characters were invented from images. Later characters were invented from ideas. Throughout the ages, the creation of new characters was sometimes done whimsically, without any reason. The example of the character for 'verbose' consists of putting four characters for 'dragon' together to form one very complicated character.

In fourth grade, I was reading the newspaper one evening and came across an article about a man, a refugee from China, who had become destitute and just couldn't take it anymore. He jumped into the water by Star Ferry in the middle of the night and was found floating the next day. In the article, there was a word I didn't know, and it was so complicated that I didn't even know how to look it up in the dictionary. This was the character:

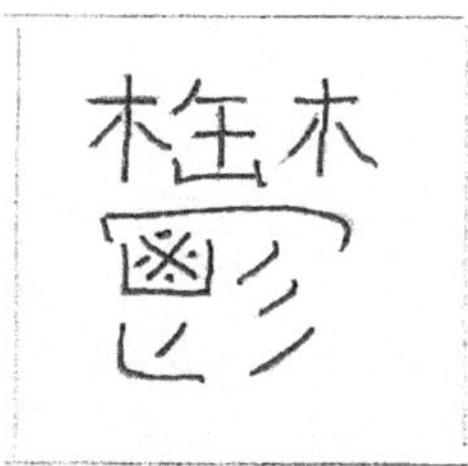

The next day I asked my teacher, and she said it was pronounced 'wat' in Cantonese and meant *depressed*. It has 30 strokes!

If you look at this character carefully, you will find that it is made up of many different components or radicals, one of which is 木 (wood) on the top left and right. By breaking down a complex character into its component parts, writing it is possible, but still not by any means easy.

Stroke Order

For a character to look correct, the strokes should be written in the proper sequence. Knowing the proper sequence will also help the writer remember the characters. The general rules of stroke order are given in the following examples.

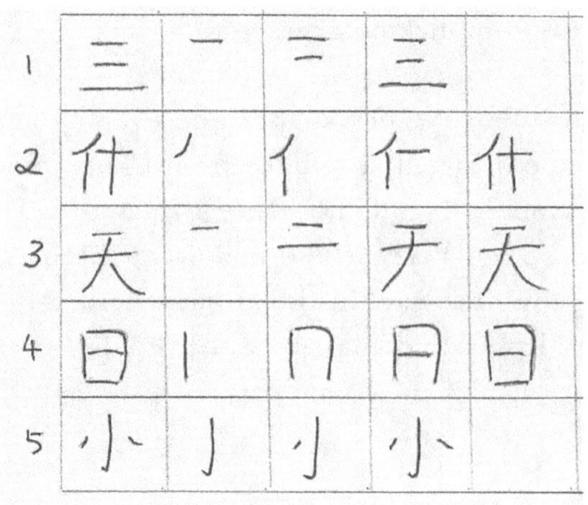

1: Top before bottom

2: Left before right

3: Horizontal before vertical/downward

4: 'Enter the room, then close the door'

5: Vertical stroke before sides/bottom

Having mastered the basic rules, we kept practicing, writing each character until we knew it. Each week we learned about ten new characters. By the time we finished the fourth grade, we would have learnt around 2,000 characters. I was able to read the newspaper and write a letter. If I didn't know a word, I could use the dictionary.

Unlike the English dictionary, just learning to use a Chinese dictionary has a high learning curve. You can use the radical—i.e., part of the character—or the number of strokes. Even for a native speaker, using the Chinese dictionary is not easy.

The village school ended in the fourth grade and students had to move on to other schools. My family decided that I would switch to an English medium school. After taking the entrance test, I was put in the fourth grade at St. Francis of Assisi in the working class neighborhood of Shum Shui Po, which was about two or three miles or a 20 minutes bus ride from my village.

At the village school, I was usually at the top of my class, with my best friend Tsang Shui Tseng sometimes taking the spot. In spite of my good grades, I was made to repeat the fourth grade because my knowledge of English was close to zero. In Hong Kong, an English medium school means that all subjects with the exception of Chinese language or Chinese history or literature would be taught in English.

At the village school, English lessons began in the fourth grade, with three periods each week. By the end of my fourth grade there, I managed to learn the alphabet but not much more. I knew the letters individually, but had yet to learn how to sound words out when the letters were put together.

I began at the St. Francis of Assisi Boys' School in September, 1956. Each day was torture, because I pretended to know more English than I did. I was in a large class with over forty pupils, and the teacher, a well-dressed, unsmiling young man who had just graduated from the Teachers' Training College, had yet to catch on to my fraud.

In my first book, *Finding Fat Lady's Shoe*, I describe how I tried to learn English on my own by writing Chinese characters with similar sounds next to the English words. For one, two, three, four and five, the corresponding Chinese words with the closest sounds were Won, Dou, Fai, Po and Hai. They just happen to mean *finding fat lady's shoe.*

The days were long at St. Francis. I was panic-stricken when Mr. Lai announced that each of us had to recite the Lord's Prayer in front of the class. Again, I applied the same system to learning it, so that 'Our Father who art in heaven' was Ou, Ah, Fa, Da, Hu, Ah, Yin, Hey, Fun and so on. I tried my best to find the Chinese words with the closest sounds, but it was impossible.

Nobody else in class seemed to have any problems, as they all had started out at St. Francis from kindergarten and thus had a much better English foundation than I did. By November, I was still floundering. The most frustrating part was that I had nobody to turn to. I couldn't tell the teacher that I wasn't following him in class. At home, nobody knew English. My father, who knew some English, was now working in Kuala Lumpur, Malaysia. It seemed like a nightmare with no end, a problem with no solution.

A year earlier, Father had been recruited by a Chinese medium school in Malaysia (formerly known as Malaya), with the plan of having the family join him once our visas were ready. It was now December, and things at St. Francis had come to a head; I had to do something, such as skipping school, because there was no way I would be able to recite the Lord's Prayer in English.

I went home one afternoon and found Mother smiling, telling me that the visas for the rest of the family were ready and we would be leaving Hong Kong by the end of the month. It was the best news I could dream of! That meant I didn't have to face my dilemma at St. Francis.

In January of 1957, I enrolled in the fourth grade at St. Andrew's School, a Catholic boys' school in Muar, Malaysia.

In the few months at St. Francis, I had learnt little English, but the situation was now different. Living in Malaysia was a total immersion experience, because unlike Hong Kong, which was, and still is, a homogenous society in which everyone speaks Cantonese, Malaysia was a multi-racial society with English as the *lingua franca*.

With constant bombardment of the language and with the help of a new friend in class named Chua Huck Cheng, who excelled in English, I soon realized that the English language was not so difficult once I learned the alphabet and knew how to pronounce the words. I read in a Chinese newspaper that in order to be a good English writer, one had to memorize the good sentences by famous writers. I began in earnest using a small notebook to write down any sentences that I thought were good and tried to memorize them. I found that the best way to become more proficient in English was to read extensively. I was fortunate that the school where my parents taught had an excellent library that was kept cool with ceiling fans. It had a large collection of English books that were seldom checked out, and also magazines from America such as *Popular Science*, *Popular Mechanics*, *Life* and *Readers' Digest.* I was overjoyed with all the excellent reading materials that were available to me and spent many hours there. The librarian was a friend of the family, and her son was a good friend of my older brother Chung. She would save the books and magazines she thought would interest me. By the time I was in the sixth grade, I was able to speak English like the rest of the boys.

Malaysia became independent on August 31, 1957, and now the Malay language was compulsory. Since I already knew the Latin alphabet, learning Malay was easy. The alphabet for the Malay language is almost identical to the English alphabet, with a few modifications. It is a simple language with few grammatical rules. For example, to make a noun plural, one just has to repeat the word, such as 'orang' (*man*), which is made plural by saying 'orang orang'.

Malaysia is so multi-racial that different groups have parallel societies with little social intercourse between them. Among the Chinese, this group is again sub-divided into different dialect groups such as Min (Fujian, or Fukien, or Hokkien), which is the majority, then the Chaochou (ChiuChao, or TeoChiu), then Yue (Cantonese), Hakka and Hanainese. The medium of instruction in the Chinese schools in Malaysia is Mandarin, which the different groups of Chinese can use to communicate with each other.

Our family lived in the teachers' quarters on campus, which was a great blessing. This meant that I was exposed to Mandarin constantly and soon learned to speak it, albeit in a Malaysian accented form. I also began to learn the other dialects out of necessity, because many of the Chinese vendors at the marketplace were uneducated and could only speak their own dialects.

In addition, I also picked up some Tamil, as there was a sizable Tamil population in Malaysia. Many of the cold drink and roasted nut vendors were Tamil, and one vendor who I made friends with taught me some of the language, especially the swear words!

By the time I was fourteen, I was able to speak and write in three languages (English, Malay and Chinese), and speak five Chinese dialects and some Tamil. Each evening after I was finished with my homework, I would read the Chinese newspaper, the only newspaper available at home at that time.

When I first began writing in my diary at age seven, I did so in Chinese. After learning English, I found that it was an easier language to write in. But when I realized that my older sister had been reading my diary, I switched to Malay, a language she didn't know!

During World War II, almost all the universities in China were closed. When the war ended, there was a severe shortage of high school teachers for the Chinese medium schools in Malaysia, which is why my parents were recruited to teach there. By 1960, many of the high school graduates from these schools had gone on to university and returned from Taiwan or the new Chinese university in Singapore, Nanyang University, with their degrees.

1960 was a bad year for my family, because my parents' contracts were not renewed and we had to return to Hong Kong. Thanks to Brother Robert, the principal of St. Andrew's School, who wrote me a wonderful letter of recommendation, I got into La Salle College (high school) in Hong Kong. There, I was placed in Form 3, i.e., 9th grade.

Having been away for five years, I had not properly studied Chinese during the entire time because I was learning English and Malay. Now I was to join the rest of the class in 9th grade level Chinese language. Chinese was considered a second language because La Salle was an English medium school.

Fortunately, my years of reading the Chinese newspaper in Malaysia had helped me remember what I had learnt in the village school, and I had most likely picked up more words along the way. A new friend in my class, Michael Sze, who happened to also live in Shatin in the New Territories, helped me with the lessons on the train each morning as we headed for school. Miraculously, I passed Chinese language as well as Chinese history and literature at the end of the school year.

After the 12th grade, I headed for the University of Hawaii. Later on in life, I was exposed to more languages such as Pidgin English in Hawaii, Spanish and French, and I have continued to enjoy learning languages throughout my life. Of all the languages I was fortunate enough to have been exposed to, Chinese has always held a strong fascination for me, with its rich and varied history and the aesthetic appeal of the character writing system.

2

Languages of the World

In order to understand the uniqueness of the Chinese language better, it would be helpful to understand how other languages work. I have included this chapter for the benefit of readers who are not familiar with the groups of world languages. They are grouped according to speech; written forms can be flexible in many languages.

The Chinese script is the only language that does not use a phonetic system (the Japanese and Korean languages adopted the Chinese script as part of their writing systems). The phonetic system has great advantages over the non-phonetic system, as one only needs to know fewer than 40 letters of any alphabet and learn the rules of that alphabet system, and one can represent in writing the sounds of any language, dialect or accent. This is how Charles Dickens was able to vividly render the accents of London in his novels and Mark Twain was able to illustrate the southern speech in America.

The problem with the non-phonetic Chinese characters is that they are analogous to the special symbols we're familiar with such as @, #, $, %, &, * and so on. These symbols represent different sounds in different languages and must be memorized through repetition. To learn to write Chinese, essentially one has to learn thousands of different symbols, most of which give no indication of how they sound. It is only through repetition that these characters can be remembered.

It is generally agreed that there are about 5,000 to 6,000 languages in the world, many of which have no written script.

Of those that have written script, most of them use the Latin and Arabic alphabets, and, to a lesser extent, the Cyrillic alphabet. Chinese is the only language that is not alphabet-based and is conceptually different from the other languages, which is why it is such a difficult language for non-native speakers to learn. It is the oldest written language that has been in use continuously. It essentially stands by itself and is not really related to any group.

A comprehensive listing of world languages is out of the scope of this book. Certain groups are only briefly mentioned while others that are more relevant to the topic of this book are discussed in more detail.

Spoken language has been around for over 100,000 years, but written language only has a history of less than 5,000 years. Almost everyone can speak one language, but many are unable to read or write. To read and write requires an active process of learning.

The human communication system is versatile. It can be transferred to writing or signs, and it can be used to discuss anything. A normal person can produce and understand an indefinite number of sentences that have never been said before. Almost any person has the potential to learn any language—including sign language for those who can't speak. A Chinese baby adopted by Israeli parents would grow up speaking fluent Hebrew—I once met one such woman.

There is strong evidence that language is an intrinsic part of being human, and the ability is biologically programmed into the species. In fact, people with mental disabilities can have perfectly normal languages skills. People with a rare genetic disorder called Williams Syndrome, which is caused by a deletion of about 25 genes from the long arm of the chromosome 7, are actually linguistically precocious. Because of the many missing genes, these individuals have many medical and neurological problems, such as gross motor difficulties. On the other hand, some people who are highly intelligent have profound difficulties with language. Albert Einstein didn't talk until he was four years old.

According to current majority opinion, language probably emerged between 100,000 and 150,000 years ago in the east of Africa. About 50,000 to 70,000 years ago, humans left Africa, probably in different waves, and moved northward into Asia Minor, then spread around the world. As our species travelled, languages split and proliferated. There are an estimated 5,000 to 6,000 languages in the world today. There is such a discrepancy in this number because sometimes it's not easy to define what a language is. For example, Cantonese is classified as a dialect, but most linguists regard it as a separate language.

The world languages are grouped into around a dozen major clusters, and a number of minor ones.

The late Joseph Greenberg, a noted linguist from Stanford University, along with a few other linguists tried to find the Proto-World language, i.e., the father of all languages, by proposing a list of twenty-seven words that they considered likely to have been used in the ancestor to all of the world's languages. But their theory has not been convincing.

The list below outlines the rough number of speakers (in millions), as first or second language, of the top twenty world languages. Exact numbers of those who speak each one as a second language are very difficult to assess, as it depends on the level of fluency of these speakers. These numbers may also vary greatly depending on the source, but the numbers here are the most current and their methodology seems most reliable. I decided to group Indonesian and Malay under one language because they are truly mutually intelligible.

Mandarin: 1,100 million (900 native and 200 as a second language)
English: 1,000 million (400 native and 600 as a second language)
Hindi: 490
Spanish: 440
Arabic: 280
Indonesian-Malay: 268
Bengali: 230
Russian: 220 (145 native and 75 as a second language)
Portuguese: 213
German: 130 (100 native and 30 as a second language)
French: 130
Japanese: 126
Urdu: 104
Vietnamese: 90
Telugu: 78
Wu (Shanghainese): 78
Tamil: 77
Cantonese: 77
Korean: 76
Turkish: 75

The world's major language groups most likely developed independently of each other. The Indo-European family is the world's largest group and includes most of the languages spoken in Europe, America and much of Asia. Latin and Greek, the two great classical languages of antiquity, belong to this group. The list below shows the different groups, subgroups and branches of the Indo-European languages. It is not possible to list all the minor languages. In Europe, only Hungarian, Basque, Finnish and Estonian (the last two are similar) are not in this group. Turkish, which we know from history was the language of a people from Central Asia who conquered Anatolia, belongs to another group.

INDO-EUROPEAN LANGUAGES

Indo-European has the following sub-groups:
Germanic
Italic
Romance
Celtic
Hellenic
Albanian
Slavic
Baltic
Armenian
Indo-Iranian

Germanic is divided into Western and Northern branches.
The western branch includes English, German, Dutch and Flemish.
The northern branch includes Swedish, Danish, Norwegian and Icelandic.

The **Italic** sub-group includes Latin.

Romance languages (languages derived from Vulgar Latin) include Italian, French, Spanish, Portuguese and Romanian. *Romance does not mean romantic, but rather that their linguistic origins were from Rome.*

Celtic is divided into Brythonic and Goidelic.
Brythonic includes Welsh; Goidelic contains Irish and Scottish. Both are Gaelic.

Hellenic includes Greek.

Albanian is an independent branch of the Indo-European language tree, spoken primarily in Greece, Italy, Kosovo, Macedonia and Montenegro.

Slavic is divided into Eastern, Western and Southern.

Eastern gave rise to Russian, Ukrainian and Belorussian.
Western gave rise to Polish, Czech and Slovak.
Southern gave rise to Bulgarian, Serbo-Croatian, Slovenian and Macedonian.

Baltic gave rise to Lithuanian and Latvian.

Armenian can be further divided into two sub-groups, Western and Eastern Armenian.

Indo-Iranian is divided into Iranian and Indic.

Iranian gave rise to Persian, Pashto, Kurdish, Tajik and Ossetian.
Indic gave rise to Sanskrit, Hindi, Urdu, Bengali, Punjabi, Marathi, Gujarati, Bihari, Rajasthani, Assamese, Kashmiri, Nepali, Sindhi and Sinhalese, etc.

Where did the Proto-Indo-European language begin? As there were no written documents, the answers to these questions were obtained by attempting to reconstruct the language. It is generally accepted that the Indo-Europeans lived in a cold northern region, among forests but not near the sea. They raised domestic animals such as the horse, cow, sheep and dog. Among the wild animals they knew were the bear and the wolf. It is believed that because of their use of the horse and cart, they were able to spread over an enormous expanse of territory.

The original Indo-European civilization is believed to have developed somewhere in Eastern Europe around 3000 BCE. Around 2500 BCE, it broke up. *(One theory is that their homeland was flooded. Genetic studies support the theory that the Indo-Europeans came from the southern Russian steppe.)* The people migrated in many different directions: some headed northward into Russia; others moved through Central Europe and reached the British Isles. Other divisions moved to Greece and into Italy; and another branch traversed Iran and Afghanistan and eventually reached India. Wherever they settled, the Indo-Europeans must have overcome the existing populations, if there were any; and later, the Indo-European language was adopted by or imposed upon the people.

The likelihood of so many languages seemingly coming from a common ancestor was first suggested in 1767 by an English physician named James Parsons. He observed that some of the relationship comes from the spread of Latin under the Roman Empire, which gave rise to the so-called 'Romance languages'. Italian, Spanish, Portuguese, French and Romanian belong to the Romance group. These languages were derived from Vulgar (common) Latin, which was spoken in Rome. Romanian is closest to Latin and its people are descendants of Roman soldiers.

Parsons' paper demonstrated the relationship between several languages by comparing the words for the number three: Irish is tri, Greek is treis, Latin is tres, French is trois, German is drei, Dutch is drei and Swedish is tre.

In 1797, an English judge in India, a noted scholar named William Jones, discussed the culture of India and the Sanskrit language, the ancient language of India, which he felt also belonged to the Indo-European language family.

By 1818, more than fifty separate languages were determined to belong to his group. Albanian was added to this list in 1854 and Armenian in 1875.

The current population of the world is around 7 billion. It is estimated that about 40% are Indo-European speakers, which would be around 3 billion people. It is the largest language group, with the widest range from Russian to Sanskrit.

Of great interest to me is the history of an ancient language called Tocharian (now extinct), which was used by a European people who had travelled to the western part of China in what is now called Xinjiang. They left writings, which helped scholars determine that it was an Indo-European language. The mummies (made possible by the dry desert conditions) of these people were noted to be tall with blond hair and blue eyes. It is quite probable that a small group of Indo-Europeans left and ended up there when their civilization collapsed around 2500 BCE (incidentally, the mummies were carbon dated to be around 4,000 to 5,000 years old). Quite a few mummies of these Indo-European people were found in several desert locations in Xinjiang near Turpan. They are now housed in the museum in Urumqi, Xinjiang.

URALIC LANGUAGES

Uralic has two subgroups:
Finno-Ugric
Samoyed

Finno-Ugric is divided into Finnic and Ugric.
The Finnic branch includes Finnish, Estonian and others.
Ugric includes Hungarian and a few minor languages.

Samoyed comprises a bunch of minor languages like Samoyed, Yurak and others.

The Uralic languages (a total of 38 languages) are spoken by about 25 million people, with the most native speakers in Hungary, Finland and Estonia.

The original home of the Proto-Uralic language speakers is believed to be in the vicinity of the Volga River about 6,000 years ago, west of the Ural Mountains in Russia, not too far from the homeland of the Proto-Indo-Europeans. About 3,000 years ago, they began migrating to lands far from their original homes, like Finland and Estonia. Others moved north and east into the lands of Western Siberia.

The term Ugric is an old Russian name for western Siberia. It was to this area that the Ugric peoples migrated, and then later began a long migration westward. Eventually they reached present-day Hungary in the 9th century. This explains the rare phenomenon of Hungarian, a language totally unrelated to the languages of its neighboring countries.

The second branch of the Uralic family consists of the four Samoyed languages. Two of them have less than 1,000 speakers.

The separation of the Finno-Ugric and Samoyed peoples is believed to have occurred more than 5,000 years ago. The Finno-Ugric groups headed west and south, while the Samoyeds headed east.

ALTAIC LANGUAGES

Altaic contains the following subgroups:
Turkic
Mongolian
Tungusic
Korean
Japanese

Turkic has several branches: Southwestern (Oghuz), Northwestern (Kipchak) and Southeastern (Chagatai).
The Southwestern branch includes Turkish, Azerbaijani and Turkmen.
The Northwestern branch includes Kazakh, Kirgiz, Tatar and Bashkir.
The Southeastern branch includes Uzbek and Uyghur.

The Mongolian group encompasses Mongolian as the main language and Buryat and Kalmyk as minor ones.

Tungusic has Northern and Southern branches.
The Northern branch includes Evenki (Tungus) and Even (Lamut).
The Southern branch includes Manchu, Xibo (Sibo) and Nanai.

Some linguists feel that **Korean** does not belong here, but most do.

Most linguists agree that **Japanese** belong to the Altaic group.

This group is named after the Altai Mountains in western Mongolia. The Altaic languages are spoken across a vast area from Turkey to the west, across Central Asia, into Mongolia and China. There are an estimated 120 million people speaking the three divisions of Turkic, Mongolian and Tungusic. Korean (60 million speakers) and Japanese (150 million speakers) are also thought to belong to the Altaic group. A few scholars feel that these two languages should be classified as independent, not belonging to any group.

The Turkic languages are homogeneous groups of about 20 languages, which are essentially mutually intelligible. Turkish accounts for about half of these speakers. The others include

Azerbaijani, Turkmen, Tatar, Uzbek, Kazakh, Kyrgyz and Uyghur.

The Mongolian branch consists primarily of Mongolian. The other languages in this group are basically dialects. Mongolian was the language of the great Mongol Empire established by Genghis Khan, which did not have a written language until Uyghur scholars used Uyghur writing to represent the Mongolian spoken language. Prior to adopting the Sogdian writing, which was used along the Silk Road, the Uyghurs themselves had no writing. The now extinct Sogdian writing is also thought to be of Indo-European origin like Tocharian.

The Tungusic languages include Sibo, which is spoken in northwestern China. Another Tungusic language is Manchu, spoken by the once great Manchu (Qing) Dynasty. The Manchu language is now considered extinct, with its people having been assimilated into Han.

These peoples were nomads and it is not possible to point to a single group living in a certain time and certain place as the progenitor of this language group. The Kyrgyz are the oldest known Turkic people.

When Genghis Khan established the Mongol Empire in the 13th century, most of the Turkic peoples fell under the domination of the Mongols. But through this process, the many Mongols adopted the Turkic languages.

Altaic languages are written in a variety of scripts: for example, Latin, Cyrillic, Arabic, Mongolian and Manchu; and some of them are written in more than one script. Many of them remain largely unwritten to this day.

In the case of the Uyghurs in Xinjiang, China, they have at different times used several scripts after they abandoned their original Sogdian-based writing. After they converted to Islam, they switched to the Arabic alphabet, then later to the Latin alphabet, and, for a time, Cyrillic (when Russia tried to hold them under its influence). They then switched back to Latin, and now use the Arabic alphabet. Interestingly, within some families, some members of different generations cannot write to each other because they were educated in different scripts!

Now, away from Russian influence, most Central Asian countries try to switch their script from Cyrillic to Latin to make it easier for the people to adapt to the changing world, especially for the use of the computer.

CAUCASIAN LANGUAGES

Caucasian has the following subgroups:
Southern: Georgian
Western: Abkhazian, etc.
Eastern: Chechen, Ingush
Dagestan: Avar, etc.

These languages are spoken in the region known as the Caucasus, which lies both north and south of the Caucasus Mountains, between the Caspian and Black Seas. This small area is now mainly in Russia and Georgia. Because of the extreme isolation, languages often vary from town to town and even from village to village. There are about 40 of them, with about 6 million speakers. Only 12 have been committed to writing.

Georgian is the dominant Caucasian language, spoken by more people than all the rest put together. The most famous speaker of this language was Joseph Stalin.

The Caucasus has had a troubled history since ancient times. It had served as a refuge for persecuted people who fled into the mountains from invaders like the Turks, Mongols, Arabs,

Romans, Macedonians and Persians. Around 1865, the area was finally incorporated into the Russian empire.

SINO-TIBETAN LANGUAGES

Sino-Tibetan has the following subgroups:
Sinitic
Tibeto-Burman
Tai
Miao-Yao

Sinitic gave rise to Chinese.
Tibeto-Burman led to Tibetan, Burmese and a number of minor languages.
Tai gave rise to Thai, Lao and a number of minor languages.
Miao-Yao led to Miao and Yao.

With over a billion Chinese speakers, this is by far the largest language group. The other major languages are Tibetan, Thai, Burmese and Lao. There are an undetermined number of lesser languages spoken in India, China, Burma, Nepal and other countries.

This group is divided into four branches, with Chinese forming a separate branch of its own.

A second branch is the Tibeto-Burman languages, which include Tibetan and Burmese, and a hundred lesser languages.

A third branch consists of the Tai languages, which include Thai and Lao as well as others.

The last branch consists of two other languages spoken in China and Southeast Asia called Miao and Yao.

It is far from certain that the languages of each of the four branches are genetically related to those of the other three. Unlike the Indo-European family, little study has been done to determine the relationships of its members. In particular, the

Chinese language bears little resemblance to the other three in the 'group' to which is belongs.

Chinese itself has been studied extensively. More studies of the other languages are needed to work out a more definitive classification.

MON-KHMER LANGUAGES

Mon-Khmer

The major language is Khmer (Cambodian), with minor languages including Mon and Palaung.

The Khmer empire was one of the great civilizations of the world. It was dominant in Southeast Asia from the 9th through the 12th century. The center of this civilization was the capital city of Angkor. Later, the Khmers were overcome by the Thais; and at the end of the 14th century their empire was destroyed and forgotten for several hundred years.

The Mon-Khmer group is derived from the two languages spoken in Southeast Asia. Khmer is the national language of Cambodia. Mon is a relatively minor language today, but at one time it was one of the most influential in the region. There are many other minor languages in this group.

DRAVIDIAN LANGUAGES

Dravidian

The major languages are Tamil, Malayalam, Telugu and Kanarese. There are a number of minor languages as well.

The Dravidian languages are dominant in southern India. About 200 million people speak a total of 20 of these languages, with

Tamil being the most widely spoken in Tamil Nadu (capital: Maras) as well as in northeastern Sri Lanka.

Malayalam is spoken in Kerala (capital: Trivandrum), while Telugu is spoken in Andhra Pradesh (capital: Hyderabad). The Dravidian languages are known to have been spoken in India before the arrival of the Indo-Europeans around 1000 BCE.

MALAYO-POLYNESIAN (AUSTRONESIAN) LANGUAGES

Malayo-Polynesian has the following branches:
Indonesian
Micronesian
Melanesian
Polynesian

Indonesian gave rise to Indonesian, Malay, Javanese, Tagalog, Ilocano, Visayan, Malagasy and many minor languages.

Micronesian gave rise to Marshallese, Yapese, Trukese and others.

Melanesian gave rise to Fijian and a few others.

Polynesian gave rise to Hawaiian, Tahitian, Maori, Samoan, Tongan, Marquesan, Rarotongan, Niuean, Uvea and Tuamotu.

This large family of languages covers more than halfway around the world, through the Indonesian archipelago, the Philippines and across the Pacific Ocean, to Madagascar off the coast of Africa. There are about 200 million speakers of this family of languages, with the majority speaking the Indonesian branch. The other three branches—Polynesian, Melanesian and Micronesian—have less than one and a half million speakers.

Indonesian is the official language of Indonesia, Malay in Malaysia, Tagalog in the Philippines and Malagasy in Madagascar.

In Indonesia, there are also a number of other languages like Javanese, Sundanese, Madurese, Achinese, Balinese and others.

In the Philippines, there are also other languages: Ilocano, Visayan, Pampangan, Igorot and others.

In Taiwan, the 300,000 aborigines speak several languages belonging to the Mayo-Polynesian family.

In Micronesia, generally north of the equator, hundreds of languages belonging to this family are spoken on countless islands across the Pacific Ocean, such as Chamorro in Guam (50,000), Gilbertese on Kiribati (50,000), Trukese on Truk and so on.

In Melanesia, south of the equator, Fijian is the most prevalent language, with about 300,000 speakers. More than a hundred other Melanesian languages are spoken in the Solomon Islands, New Guinea, New Caledonia and Vanuatu.

Generally, the Polynesian languages spread across the Pacific Ocean east of the International Date Line. From west to east, there are the Maori of New Zealand with about 300,000 speakers, Samoan with about 255,000, Tongan with 110,000, Tahitian with 200,000, Marquesan with 10,000, and off the coast of South America, Easter Island has about 6,000 speakers. The Hawaiian Islands north of the equator have recently undergone a renaissance of the Polynesian-based Hawaiian language, and each year more locals are learning to speak the language, which was almost extinct a few decades ago. In spite of this, it's difficult to assess how many of them actually use it in everyday communication.

Most of the Polynesian languages have a certain degree of mutual intelligibility. The settlement of the islands in the Pacific probably began around 1500 BCE. Recent genetic studies have traced the most likely original homeland of these people to Taiwan. The aborigines in Taiwan were known to be good seafarers, which would explain how they managed to find all the small islands across the Pacific Ocean!
There is strong evidence that all these languages belong to the same group. Growing up in Malaysia, I learnt to speak the Malay language, and when I went to Hawaii for university, I noted many similar words between the Hawaiian and the Malay languages. Of interest is that in almost all these languages, five is 'lima', while there are variations in the other numbers.

PAPUAN LANGUAGES

The Papuan languages are spoken mainly on New Guinea, with some extension into the Solomon Islands and New Britain. There are more than 500 of these languages spoken by only about 2 million people. These languages show such wide variations among themselves that they don't seem to belong to a single family. Some of the languages have only a few hundred speakers.

The interior of the huge island is one of the least accessible regions on the planet. Some of the inhabitants still live in Stone Age conditions. Often, two villages separated by a valley will speak mutually unintelligible languages.

AUSTRALIAN LANGUAGES

These languages refer to those spoken by the aborigines in Australia. There are several hundred different languages spoken by less than 100,000 people.

The aborigines inhabited Australia for tens of thousands of years before Western influence was introduced and had plenty of time to develop their own languages in different parts of the continent. It is unlikely that these languages form a single family, but there are certain words that are similar in every language.

Aranda is the most prevalent language and is spoken in the center of the continent. Words like boomerang, kangaroo, koala and wallaby are Arandan words.

PALEO-ASIATIC LANGUAGES

These are a number of minor languages spoken in eastern and northern Siberia. They have no genetic link with each other or with any linguistic family.

Chukchi is the most significant of the Paleo-Asiatic languages. It is spoken by about 12,000 people in the part of Siberia nearest Alaska.

Some linguists also include Eskimo and Aleut languages in this family. Some also add Ainu, spoken in Japan. However, there is no genetic relationship between these languages.

Despite the tiny numbers of speakers of these languages, the Soviet authorities devised Cyrillic-based alphabets for Chukchi, Koryak and Nivkh.

ESKIMO-ALEUT LANGUAGES

There are only two languages in this group.

Eskimo is spoken by about 100,000 people in Siberia, Alaska, Canada and Greenland.

Aleut is spoken by about 2,000 people in the Aleutian Islands. These two languages are related to each other but are vastly different, as they obviously diverged several thousand years ago.

The languages of the African continent deserve a much more extensive section, but it is beyond the scope of this book.

NIGER-CONGO LANGUAGES

This very large group of languages includes some that we are familiar with such as Swahili, Ruanda, Kikuyu, Swazi, Zulu, Xhosa and Banda.

This group of languages extends from Senegal in westernmost Africa, across to Nigeria, and then down the southern half of the continent as far as South Africa.

AFRO-ASIATIC LANGUAGES

The **Afro-Asiatic group** contains the following branches:
Semitic: North Arabic: Arabic, Maltese
Canaanitic: Hebrew
Aramaic: Syriac, Aramaic and Assyrian
Ethiopic: Amharic, Tigrinya, Tigre and others
Berber: Tuareg and others
Cushitic: Somali and others
Egyptian: Coptic
Chadic: Hausa

These five branches of Afro-Asiatic languages are spoken by about 300 million people with very different racial, religious and cultural origins. There is little doubt among authorities that they are interrelated.

The Semitic languages can be traced back some 5,000 years. Arabic was originally a minor language in the Arabian Peninsula. With the rise of Islam in the 7th century, it spread all the way across North Africa to the Atlantic Ocean.

It was the Semitic people who first used the alphabet. The Phoenicians began using it around the 15th century BCE, and later, the Hebrews borrowed the Phoenician writing. The Greeks adopted this alphabet around 1000 BCE, which later spread to many regions of the world.

CHARI-NILE LANGUAGES

This group of languages is spoken in the Sudan, Uganda, Kenya and Chad, and to a lesser extent in regions adjacent to these countries. About 25 million people speak this group of languages.

One of the languages belonging to this group is Nubian, which is spoken in the Nile Valley of the Sudan. Another language in this group that you may have heard of is the Masai language of Kenya and Tanzania.

KHOISAN LANGUAGES

We are familiar with the Khoisan languages because of the distinctive feature of the so-called click consonants, made by drawing air into the mouth and clicking the tongue. The most prevalent of these is Bushman, with about 100,000 speakers. About 75,000 speak Hottentot.

The term Khoisan is composed of the word 'Khoi' which is the Hottentot word they use to refer to themselves, and 'San' is the Hottentot word for Bushman.

The languages of the Americas also deserve a larger section, but again, it is beyond the scope of this book.

NATIVE AMERICAN LANGUAGES

The American Indian language group consists of over 1,000 languages. Some are spoken by small tribes of no more than a few thousand. Over one hundred languages are spoken in the US and Canada, over 300 in Mexico and Central America and around a thousand in South America. There are about 20 million Native Americans.

In North America, there are about 50 different language families, which in turn have been grouped into super-families. Navajo, spoken in the Southwest, is now the most widely spoken Native American language in the US. Cherokee is spoken in Oklahoma and North Carolina. Seneca and Mohawk are spoken in New York. The Siouan languages include Sioux, Dakota and Crow, and are spoken mainly in the northern Midwest. The Muskogean family includes Choctaw, Chickasaw and Creek, spoken mainly in Oklahoma. The Uto-Azetecan family includes Pima and Hopi, which are spoken mainly in the Southwest.

The two once-great civilizations of Aztec and Maya were located in Mexico. Nahuatl, the Aztec language, is still widely spoken in the states adjacent to Mexico City.

The Native Americans were believed to have come from Asia across the land bridge that spanned the Bering Strait as long as 25,000 years ago. These migrations occurred most likely in small numbers over a long period of time. These people probably differed from each other in customs, languages and even physical appearance, and eventually inhabited the entire hemisphere.

Almost all the states in the Midwest of the US derived their names from an Indian language. Minnesota means *sky-blue waters* in Sioux and Oklahoma means *red-people* in Choctaw.

Of great interest is that during WWII, the US Army used Navajo for code, which the Japanese could not break. In World War I, Cherokee and Chactow were used.

INDEPENDENT LANGUAGES

Some languages do not belong to any family and are unrelated to any other languages.
Vietnamese is one, but it is related to Muong, a minor language in Vietnam.
Basque of northeastern Spain and southwestern France is also unrelated to any languages.

Barushaski, spoken in northwestern Kashmir, and **Ainu**, spoken in Hokkaido, Japan, are also unrelated to any other languages.

Some linguists feel that Japanese and Korean are also independent, but most agree that they belong to the Altai family.

PIDGIN and CREOLE LANGUAGES

These languages emerge to bridge the gap between people who otherwise could not communicate with each other.

A pidgin language usually has a markedly reduced vocabulary of a dominant language such as English or French, with some native words added. A pidgin language has no native speakers, i.e., it is spoken in addition to one's mother tongue. When pidgin eventually becomes the mother tongue of a group of people, it is then called a creole language.

Even though there are thousands of languages worldwide, many of them share common bonds. For those that aren't solely oral languages, almost all of them utilize a form of phonetic system for their written script, because it is most versatile. In spite of its relation to the larger Sino-Tibetan family of languages, the Chinese written language stands alone. Because it is so different from a phonetic system, learning it is a real challenge and studying it can be truly fascinating.

3

Overview of the Chinese Language

A recent article in the *Economist* magazine claims that Mandarin may be overtaking English as the world language. There has been tremendous interest in learning the Chinese language all over the world. The Chinese government is funding many projects, such as the Confucius Institute, to promote the Chinese language; and even some primary schools in major US and European cities are teaching Chinese.

Chinese is one of the most difficult languages to learn because of its unique and complex writing system. Because it's not an alphabet-based language, there is no system a student can rely on, and it has to be learnt by rote memory. The ratio of effort to effect is often disappointing and can be a source of frustration. If you are a college student considering taking Chinese as a second language, you should be aware of this. It may be more work than you bargained for. But if you are a retiree and wish to have a hobby that challenges your brain, studying Chinese may be a good choice. It is estimated that one needs to know the minimum of 2,000 characters to read some basic texts. It is generally accepted that there are 50,000 characters in the Chinese language.

Looking at a character would give you no idea what it should sound like. Alternately, if you only knew the sound of a character, you wouldn't have any clue how it should be written. *Pinyin* or Romanization of the Chinese characters has been adopted to help non-native speakers learn Chinese. This will be discussed in detail in the next chapter.

Some students take Chinese in school because they think it could help them succeed at work or in business later, since it is spoken by a billion people. It's true that it is spoken by a billion people, but they are almost all in China. As far as helping them at work or in business, the truth of the matter is that many educated Chinese speak some English. Depending on one's interest and aptitude, learning Chinese can be a source of joy or frustration.

As a native speaker, and learning it when I was young, Chinese was not difficult for me. Our human brain is wired to learn to communicate. As I mentioned earlier, even those with very low IQs learn to talk. But writing began only a few thousand years ago. There is a big difference between learning to speak Chinese and learning to write it. Most linguists agree that learning to speak Chinese is not much more difficult than learning to speak, say, French for a speaker of a European language. But to learn to write Chinese, most agree that it is three or four times more difficult.

As a child, I was ready to learn to write. It was my job, and there were few distractions. In contrast, studying it as a second language as an adult takes a great deal more effort to learn the 2,000 characters required to be literate.

Even knowing the 2,000 characters, a non-native speaker would find it difficult to read something like a newspaper because of the lack of cultural context. As with most languages, a native speaker knows the subtleties and contexts of the language that will aid their comprehension better than a non-native speaker, even if both know the exact same 2,000 characters.

For years, I would write home to my parents weekly from Hawaii and was able to describe in detail what I was doing in college, my feelings and my new environment. Then I went into medicine, lived in America for decades and no longer wrote Chinese on a regular basis. Now, sadly, if I have to write a simple letter, it takes me hours to look up characters I've forgotten, and even then I know it's obvious that the letter is written by a person with no more than a high school education. This has happened to many of my friends who were once educated in the Chinese language. Chapter 17 is *Amnesia and the Chinese Language*, which will discuss the subject in more detail.

Most Chinese educators have long realized that it takes the average Chinese student two more years to be proficient in the Chinese language compared to their European counterparts in their own languages. In addition, retaining what one has learnt has always been a problem with the Chinese written language. At the beginning of the 20th century, when China was behind in its development, many Chinese intellectuals actually believed Charles Darwin's theory that the Chinese were lagging behind their Western counterparts and were intellectually inferior. They could not understand how ancient China, once so advanced in science, having developed the compass, gunpowder, papermaking and printing, was now so hopelessly backward.

Many were convinced that the language was the problem. In the early 1900s, few people in China could read. Not only was it difficult for the masses to learn enough characters to be literate, but adding to the dilemma was that writing Chinese required a classical style called Wen Yen, and even fewer Chinese could write or comprehend it. In high school, I can vividly recall teachers having to explain the meaning of passages written in the classical style. They had to be interpreted by scholars first. There was no way I could make any sense of those passages on my own, even though I recognized almost all of the characters.

Early in the 20th century, the situation seemed so desperate that a group of intellectuals proposed that the Chinese speech and writing system be replaced by Esperanto or some other foreign language. The proposal was of course rejected as impossible. Others suggested that the speech be retained and used as the basis of a new writing system based on the Latin alphabet. Later, some Soviet linguists tried to convince the Chinese to use the Cyrillic alphabet for the written language as they had done with all of their Central Asian Turkic speaking republics.

In the end, the reform was to make the written language match how it was spoken. But the masses still had to learn thousands of characters.

To add to the conundrum, now there are two writing systems. Since it takes so long for someone to become literate in the Chinese language, the government decided early in the 20th century to simplify some of the characters in order to make it easier for the masses to learn. Now, in Mainland China the simplified version is used, while the traditional form is still used in Hong Kong, Taiwan and many Southeast Asian countries. It is extremely difficult for me to read anything in simplified characters. I have to do it slowly, and often have to guess at what some of the characters are. Sometimes I have absolutely no idea what original characters are being represented by the simplified forms, such as in the case of the name of Hong Kong and Shanghai Bank:

匯 豐 This is the traditional form.

汇 丰 This is the simplified version.

There is no way that I would have guessed it. To me, the simplified version may as well be Japanese!

The existence of two forms of writing complicates things for everyone, especially new learners. Computers have to deal with two characters sets. The traditional characters, using more strokes and thus more ink, have a denser look. The simplified characters have a cleaner look with more open space. The traditional characters in Taiwan and Hong Kong are usually printed in the traditional format, with lines running down the page, from right to left. On the Mainland, simplified characters are printed across the page from left to right and are read from top to bottom, just as in English.

People in Hong Kong and Taiwan find the simplified characters unattractive and difficult to read. Even in Mainland China, many people find the older forms of writing more attractive. Despite a resurgence of traditional characters on the Mainland, the simplified forms are here to stay, and it is unlikely that the government would ever revert back to the traditional form.

For the masses, perhaps the simplified form is better because there are fewer strokes and it can be written faster. But many feel that they're losing a great part of the Chinese culture by changing something that has been around for thousands of years.

Traditional Chinese writing is a beautiful language and I am glad that I was once proficient in it and can still read most common texts. But it is not a practical writing system, and I don't think it is compatible with the changing world. It is the only writing system that is not alphabet-based, with the exception of Japanese. But even Japanese has a parallel system that is similar to an alphabet, which is supplemented with some Chinese characters. This will be discussed in a separate chapter.

Is Chinese a primitive or an advanced language?

In 1681, French scholar De Vienne Plancy thought the Chinese writing system was so superior that he wrote to fellow scholars and said he was surprised that Chinese characters had not been adopted throughout the world, since they immediately signify ideas. For a time, scholars debated just how to utilize the universal quality attributed to Chinese characters. They equated the Chinese system to the Arabic numeral system, which, no matter what language a person uses, always represent the same idea. This is clearly not the case with other language systems: for example, the number 5 in English is *five*, in Spanish it is *cinco*, in Mandarin it is *wu*, in Hawaiian it is *elima*, and so on. Scholars were impressed that through the Chinese character system of writing, two educated people who couldn't understand a word the other spoke were able to communicate with each other through writing.

Some scholars were even more impressed that a Chinese character could be understood in Japan, Korea and Vietnam, even though the countries have totally different languages. These countries adopted this system of writing over a thousand years ago. Japanese still uses Chinese characters. The two Koreas now use their own alphabet system but retain Chinese characters for some functions. Vietnam has completely eliminated Chinese characters and has adopted through the French a modified Latin alphabet.

Other scholars felt that Chinese actually represented a higher degree of linguistic development because it did not use unnecessary features like conjugations and gender identification that were retained in varying degrees by European languages. They thought that Chinese grammar was easier without the complex verb conjugation, agreement of nouns and adjectives, and other features of European languages that Chinese didn't employ.

For a while, many of the best minds in Europe were convinced that the best system was one in which, as John DeFrancis puts it in *The Chinese Language: Fact and Fantasy*, 'the characters represented meaning without regard to sound and...a single character was ascribed to a single thing, whether abstract or concrete'. They tried to develop a universal language based on the Chinese system. Numerous schemes were created, but, without exception, they were rejected as their inadequacies became apparent.

The obvious reason for the failure of the various systems proposed is that it is simply impossible to classify all things known in tables so that each item would be assigned its own universal character. In addition, any system of writing not based on actual speech simply doesn't work. Our brains are wired for speaking, but writing requires active learning and memory. Trying to remember tens of thousands of characters without reference to a spoken language is virtually impossible.

Yet for all its complexity, the Chinese language is primitive in that it does not work well in the scientific age, and especially now in the digital age. Many educators and students believe that the two extra years required to learn Chinese could be better used to acquire more meaningful and useful information.

Not only that, but the regression rate of a learned language was noted to be much higher among Chinese students. Several studies in both China and Japan revealed that two years after graduation from high school, the students who did not continue with higher education had forgotten at least 20% of the characters they once knew, and in some cases, many more.

Another possible negative aspect of the Chinese writing system is that it is believed to deprive students of creativity (although there is no evidence to support this claim), because so much effort and time are spent on learning these thousands of characters, whereas their European counterparts only have to know the 26 letters in the alphabet.

Chinese is an amazing language, but the world has changed tremendously since the ideograms were invented. All other languages have moved to the alphabet system. From my personal experience, having learnt several languages, I feel that the character writing system is cumbersome and impractical compared to English or Spanish or any alphabet-based language.

Chinese is also a primitive language in that it is the oldest continuous written language used with essentially the same basic ideas as when it was first invented. Other pictogram systems like Sumerian moved on to become alphabet systems. On the contrary, however, Chinese has also been seen at some points in history to be an advanced system. It is certainly not primitive that the pictograms have become ideograms that are part of a complicated system of some 50,000 characters with its limited phonetic system. (Chapter 9 will demonstrate that the Chinese language is phonetic in a limited way.) Ultimately, it is paradoxically both primitive and advanced.

4

What is Pinyin?

The most difficult part about learning Chinese is the characters. As mentioned previously, *Pinyin* is the Romanization of Chinese characters based on their pronunciation in Mandarin—a dialect spoken around Beijing, which has for centuries been used as the *lingua franca* for China's numerous mutually unintelligible dialects. It transcribes the sounds of the Chinese characters using a modified Latin alphabet.

Here is an example of Pinyin: 'ni hao' means *hello* and is the sound of these two Chinese characters: **你 好**. Literally, **你** (ni) means *you* and **好** (hao) means *well* or *good*.

Pinyin is most commonly used in China for teaching children to read. It is now also widely used by non-native speakers of Mandarin to learn the language. The word literally translates into *spell sound*. By using a familiar system—the Latin alphabet—one learns an unfamiliar system—the Chinese characters.

Historically, the Japanese were the first to utilize a similar method, which they call *Romaji* (Roman letters), to help Westerners learn Japanese. Japanese also contains many Chinese characters, called *Kanji*.

Without Pinyin, learning the Chinese characters becomes much more difficult. Even if one has learned how to write Mandarin, there is no way to know how it sounds. Pinyin solves that problem.

The Pinyin system may seem confusing at first because the words are not pronounced as they are in the English alphabet, and there are some combinations of letters that do not exist in English such as 'xi', 'qie' and 'cui'. 'C' in Pinyin is pronounced like the 'ts' sound in 'grits' as opposed to 'k' in English. English alphabet rules should be discarded when using the Pinyin system. If one is serious about learning Mandarin, the Pinyin system should be followed closely; otherwise, it will lead to confusion and frustration.

Adding to the difficulty, there are four tones in Mandarin that help to clarify the meanings in words:

ー	ˊ	ˇ	ˋ
Tone 1	Tone 2	Tone 3	Tone 4
High level	High rising	Low dipping	High falling

The tone symbols are written over the nuclear vowel in a syllable such as in jiā, méi, hǎo and kuài.

To add to the confusion, some syllables are distinguished by absence of tone. They have a neutral tone and are said to be atonic, such as in the word 蚊子 or wénzi (*mosquito*), which differs in pronunciation from 文 字 or wénzì (*writing*) because of its neutral tone on the second syllable! One must speak clearly and listen very carefully in Chinese.

The following is the most commonly used example to demonstrate the four tones:

媽 mā tone 1 means *mother*

麻 má tone 2 means *hemp*

馬 mǎ tone 3 means *horse*

罵 mà tone 4 means *to scold*

There are many funny stories about situations that arise when the wrong tones are used. Improper tones can result in entirely different words, as in the following:

Shuǐ jiǎo means *dumpling* and the characters are 水 餃, but shuì jiào means *sleep*, and is of course made up of totally different characters (睡 覺).

Before you order dumplings in a restaurant, make sure you get the tones right!

Some characters sound exactly the same, with the same tone and spelling, but with different meanings. For example,

Zhū 豬 means *pig*, but
Zhū 珠 means *pearl*.

The tones are what give Chinese speech its singsong quality and must be differentiated from intonation. Intonation can also occur in tonal languages.

Tone signs are difficult to use and are often not used in Western publications; they are also usually missing from street signs.

Pinyin has become extremely useful, as it is the most popular way to type out Chinese characters on a typical keyboard. It is used in telegraphic codes, Braille for the blind, finger spelling for the deaf, dictionaries and indexes. Pinyin is now the official Romanization system of China, Singapore, the US Library of Congress and the American Library Association. It allows easier access to documents by making it simpler to locate Chinese language materials.

It replaced the traditional writing systems of several ethnic minorities in China and has been used to document the previously unwritten languages of many more.

Pinyin is far from perfect because it uses many letter combinations unknown in English and other languages. But so far it is the best system available. Before the official adoption of Pinyin, the differing Romanization systems created confusion around the pronunciation of Chinese words. How many different spellings of Mao Zedong and Chiang Kai-shek have you come across in your reading?

Will Pinyin eventually lead to the demise of the characters? This question will be explored later in the book.

5

Comparing Chinese to the English Language

Note for this chapter: A phoneme *is the smallest distinct unit of sound in a specified language that distinguishes one word from another, for example, p, b, d, and t in the English words pad, pat, bad and bat.*

A friend once asked me, 'Since you know both languages so well, can you compare them?' The truth is that it's difficult to compare such vastly different languages, like comparing apples to oranges. However even apples and oranges share some similarities, as do the two languages.

Nowadays, China is playing an increasingly significant role in world politics and economies. It was recently reported by the *Economist* that there are now over one million Chinese nationals in the various countries of Africa, doing business or participating in programs of assistance, such as building and staffing hospitals and clinics. Recently, I was in Samoa volunteering at the government hospital. The capital, Apia, was full of Chinese workers who had just completed construction of the large hospital and the government (parliament) building, and who were staying on to build the national stadium, all courtesy of the Chinese government. A reporter from the English newspaper, *the Samoan Observer*, even compared the Chinese to the old British Empire, which had influences and economic interests in countries all over the world.

Dr. Linden, a physician in the ER department at the Apia hospital, once asked me if I thought Chinese would replace English as the common language of the world. I replied that I didn't think so because Chinese is such a difficult language to learn, and its use is really limited to China. Anyone conducting business in the world would most likely learn English, as I had noticed with the many Chinese owners of small shops throughout Samoa. These Chinese immigrants are learning English, rather than the Samoans learning Chinese. In spite of many scholarships given to African and other developing countries for their students to study at universities in China, many still cannot speak fluent Chinese, let alone write it. In fact, in medical schools and science and engineering courses at some Chinese universities, classes are conducted in English in order to attract international students.

Mandarin is spoken by almost a billion people, but the speakers are mostly in China. English is the third most common native language in the world, but it is the most common second language and is spoken all over the world. Essentially, it has assumed the role of the universal language.

English is part of the large family of Indo-European languages, whereas Chinese, even though classified as part of the Sino-Tibetan language group, is fundamentally unrelated to any other language. A few other languages are thought to be related to Chinese, but most linguists agree that this is because it was adopted by other cultures. Like most languages, both English and Chinese are bound to their culture, history and people.

Around 500 CE, the native Celtic languages of what eventually became Britain were pushed aside by the Germanic languages, which were written in runes (an ancient Germanic alphabet). With the advent of Christianity in the British Isles, the Roman alphabet was adopted. Then, in 1066, England was invaded by the Normans, bringing with them a German-French language that was mostly used by the aristocracy. Slowly, this language became popular. When the Renaissance arrived, the English appropriated many words with Latin and Greek influence. With so many foreign vowels sounds, the spelling of many words simply didn't correspond to their sounds. Even within any one of these languages, it was impossible to guarantee internal consistency. When these systems mix together haphazardly, it becomes English. It is one of the most widely spoken languages on the planet, yet it is the only language among the top ten most spoken that does not have an official regulatory academy to approve spelling.

In 1906, attempts were made in the US to make things more predictable. Words that end in –re were changed to –er, switching *sabre* to *saber*, for example. The list also eliminated the silent e in words like *abridg(e)ment* and removed silent u letters in words such as *hon(u)or* and *colo(u)r. Cheque* became *check*. But when an attempt was made to change *through* into *thru*, it simply did not catch on because the habit of using *through* was too entrenched.

Unlike the shifting English language, Chinese is an old language that has not undergone many major changes. The concepts are still the same as they were 4,000 years ago.

The first Chinese writing, called Oracle Bone Script, was discovered on ox scapula and turtle shells dating from around 1500 BCE. Later Chinese writing can, in many cases, be traced directly to the pictograms of Oracle Bone Script. In the case of the English language, it has undergone so many transformations over the centuries that it is nearly impossible for the present-day reader to read Old English.

English is written horizontally starting at the top of the page, from left to right. Traditionally, Chinese writing most often appears in vertical columns and is read from the top down, starting from the right to the left. However, Chinese can be written horizontally like English as well. Because Chinese is made up of individual characters and not an alphabet, it doesn't really matter which direction it is written in, because at a glance, the reader can quickly decide which direction makes sense. English written in any other direction than left to right wouldn't make sense, for obvious reasons. The characters of the alphabet don't stand alone to create meaning.

The biggest difference between the two languages is that Chinese is tonal while English is not. A Chinese language syllable pronounced with a rising tone may have a very different meaning from the same syllable without the rising tone. In English one usually finds a rising tone at the end of a question, which can alter the context, but not the individual meaning of each word.

It has been observed that English speakers have an easier time with the tones in Chinese than other Europeans such as the French, Spanish, and German, even though the German and French can vocalize the vowel 'ü' that the English often find difficult. Usually after some practice, most English speakers can master the tones. *I am not sure if this means English has sounds closer to Chinese than the other European languages or if the English are quicker learners!*

I have been asked if it would it be easier for an English speaker to learn to speak Chinese or the other way around. In my opinion, it would be easier for an English speaker to learn Chinese than for a Chinese speaker to learn English. To speak Chinese, one just has to learn new words with little worry for the grammar, whereas the Chinese speaker learning to speak English has to worry about the syntax, tenses, plurals, he/she and on and on. But learning the writing is just the opposite. It would take an English learner many years to master the 2,000 or so Chinese characters just to be able to read basic texts.

Written Chinese is very difficult for most people, as it is extremely detail oriented and memory intensive. This form of writing is the only writing system China has ever used throughout its long history. During much of the last few thousand years, people did not move around, and regional dialects became so diversified that they became unintelligible to each other. If the language used an alphabet system, it would have caused chaos, because every dialect would have different sounds for their words; thus, every word would be spelled differently, making communication impossible between the regions. Traditional Chinese characters have the same meaning in all dialects. Therefore, the pronunciation may be different, but the written meaning is clear.

An American friend once told me that when he began learning Chinese characters, he felt like a child playing *spot-the-difference* in the Sunday paper, a puzzle where the reader searches for tiny differences in two almost identical pictures.

Take the two characters below for example:

特 持

The first is 'te' which means *special*. The second is 'chi' which means *grasp*. The first has a tiny extra stroke on the top left hand side, whereas the latter has a tiny upward tick at the bottom of the long vertical stroke. You can see why English speakers learning Chinese need to rewire their brains to recognize small differences between the many characters. Chinese reading uses more of the frontal part of the left hemisphere of the brain (called the left middle frontal region), whereas reading languages with an alphabet uses a posterior part of the brain (the left temporo-parietal region).

It is well known that many students from East Asia who have studied English for many years, and who can read English texts, either cannot speak it or they speak it poorly. On the contrary, many Westerners who have learnt to speak Mandarin cannot read it. It is also true that a Westerner may be able to speak Mandarin but still have a difficult time watching movies in the language because so many words sound the same. Imagine trying to differentiate shùxué (*mathematics*) from shūxuě (*blood transfusion*) and guòjiǎng (*you flatter me*) from guǒjiàng (*fruit paste* or *jam*)!

As discussed earlier, as we enter adulthood, it becomes increasingly difficult to learn a second language. One of the reasons is that our brains become hardwired to speak that one language. This is why some East Asians have such a hard time speaking English clearly; in the East Asian languages, the 'r' and 'l' sounds are usually not distinguished. The story about waiters in Chinese restaurants asking you if you want more 'lice' is true!

Sound units of words are called *phonemes*. Studies suggest that as the language center of our brain matures, certain phonemes are 'wired' into those areas. Since the Chinese language does not distinguish between 'r' and 'l', a single phoneme represents both sounds. When a Chinese speaker is presented with English words containing either of these sounds, brain-imaging studies show that only a single region in the brain is activated. In native English speakers, imaging shows different areas of activation for each sound. For a Chinese speaker, distinguishing 'r' and 'l' would require a rewiring of certain elements of the brain's circuitry. This is also true for 'd' and 't'. The Chinese cannot differentiate the two.

Studies have shown that by 6 to 10 months old, children have already learned to be sensitive to the basic sounds (phonemes) that matter in their native language. Other studies have gone further to prove that sound recognition begins with the fetus in the womb. By the time babies are born, they already have definite preferences for the sounds they are used to hearing. Chinese and English differ profoundly in the sounds they use, and the brain tends to reject sounds it doesn't need. If, later on in life, one decides to learn another language, the brain would have to learn to recognize unfamiliar phonemes.

Even something as simple as learning the English alphabet correctly is a difficult task for Chinese speakers. This is because there are many sounds in the alphabet that are unfamiliar to a Chinese speaking person. In Chinese, each character has a single phoneme. To say the letter 'f ', a Chinese speaker would break it into two phonemes and pronounce it 'ai fu'. For 'l' they would say 'ai le', 'r' would be 'ai er', and 'w' would break down into four phonemes: 'dou bei er wei'. So you can see why it's so difficult to learn English if one hasn't mastered the alphabet. It can be confusing to understand how you can string together some letters like W, H, E, R and E and come up with the pronunciation of 'where'. In spite of the English language being an alphabet-based language that is supposed to be phonetic, we all know that many English words aren't pronounced as they are spelled, and sometimes it's impossible to sound them out. When I was learning English, I had a great deal of difficulty with the pronunciation of the word 'island'; I just could not understand why the 's' wasn't pronounced.

English has many more vowel sounds than Chinese. This can cause faulty pronunciation of words like it/eat, ship/sheep and full/fool. Even after speaking the English language for so many years, I still find myself making such mistakes. The challenges of pronouncing individual English words correctly, complicated by problems with intonation, often result in the heavily accented English of some Chinese learners. Even if they have perfect grammar, their speech can still be difficult to understand.

As the Chinese language does not have any tenses, the concept of time is handled through the use of specific time words such as *yesterday*, *this morning*, or *tomorrow*. The English verb system is a major hurdle for the Chinese speaker trying to learn English.

Here are some typical verb/tense mistakes:

- I wish I am rich. (I wish I were rich.)
- I will call you as soon as I will get there. (I will call you as soon as I get there.)
- What do you do? (What are you doing?)
- She has got married last Sunday. (She got married last Sunday.)

English commonly expresses shades of meaning with verb moods, such as the increasing degree of politeness in the following instructions:

- Open the door, please.
- Could you open the door, please?
- Would you mind opening the door, please?

Chinese learners are not accustomed to verb moods, and may seem rude when making requests or suggestions.

There are some differences in word order between Chinese and English, but generally, both languages use: subject/verb/object as in 'I read a book.' However, asking a question in Chinese is conveyed by intonation. The subject and verb are not inverted as in English.

Interference from Chinese can lead to the following typical problems:

- When you are going to school?
- Chinese is a very hard to learn language.

The almost boundless English vocabulary is difficult for the Chinese to manage, especially the short verbs that commonly combine with particles to form what are known as phrasal verbs, such as: *look up to*, *take on*, *give in*, *make do* and *look down on*. Such a word use feature does not exist in Chinese and can cause great confusion.

Just as a native Chinese speaker's brain needs rewiring to learn the phonemes of the English alphabet, an English speaker's brain need rewiring to learn to differentiate the tones of the Chinese language. English speakers are familiar with tones in a different way, such as asking, 'Where have you been?' in various tones that convey surprise, anger, suspicion, jealousy, or concern.

Many English speakers learning Chinese appreciate the fact that Chinese does not have any singular or plural. The problem is that everything is counted with counting words, or 'measure' words, such as two flocks of geese and a herd of deer. The Chinese language has tons of these measure words, which can be a headache for beginners. The word for *book* or *books* is 'ben'; the measure word before it would determine whether it was one *ben* (book) or multiple *ben* (books).

Here are more examples of measure words, and there are hundreds of them:

一杯茶 yi bei cha, a cup of tea
一壶水 yi hu shui, a kettle of water
一鍋飯 yi guo fan, a pot of rice
一瓶酒 yi ping jiu, a bottle of wine

一包煙 yi bao yan, a package of cigarettes

A unique feature of the Chinese language is the repetition of words (characters) to add to or complement the meaning of the first character. Some verbs, when repeated, give the action a subtle additional nuance of meaning, such as *for a while*, *take time to*, *for now*, etc. In these cases, the tone of the repeated character changes to a lighter, softer tone.

For example:
谢谢 xiè xie, with the first character the fourth tone, and the second character a neutral tone, means *thank you.* 谢 alone means *to thank*.
听听 tīng ting means *listen for a while*. Ting 听 by itself is *to listen*.
看看 kàn kan, means *have a look* or *take a look*.
想想 xǐang xiang, means *think over for a while*.
坐坐 zùo zuo, means *sit for a while*.
走走 zǒu zou means *take some time to walk*.

Some nouns may be repeated with little change in the meaning except to add intimacy or informality. In most cases, the repeating character is changed to a lighter tone.

爸爸 bà ba = Daddy, Dad
媽媽 mā ma = Mom
哥哥 gē ge = elder brother
姊姊 jǐe jie = elder sister
弟弟 dì di = younger brother
妹妹 mèi mei = younger sister

In other cases, when the same noun character is repeated, it becomes plural to mean all or every. There is usually no change of tone in the second character.

Such as:
人人 rén rén = every person, everyone
家家 jīa jīa = every family
男男 nán nán = every male
女女 nǔ nǔ = every female
天天 tīan tīan = everyday, day after day
事事 shì shì = all the work, everything (to do)

Adjectives can also be repeated to enhance the expression. The second syllable always has the same tone as the first.

紅紅 hóng hóng = quite red, fairly red
黑黑 hēi hēi = quite black, fairly black
清清 qīng qīng = rather clear
白白 bái bái = quite white, fairly white
清清白白 qīng qīng bái bái = innocent, without sin, humble

It is true that basic sentence structure for Chinese is like the English—subject-verb-object—but in Chinese the rules are much less stringent. The meaning of a sentence often depends on the word order. Most Chinese readers will understand the word order, even though it can seem arbitrary and confusing to English readers.

The following are sentences made up of six Chinese characters with variations in character order that result in different meanings.

小 牛 山 上 吃 草
little cow hill on eat grass
(xiao niu shan shang chi cao)

1: **小牛山上吃草**
The little cow eats grass on the hill.

2: **小牛吃山上草**
Little cow eats hill on grass (meaning the little cow eats grass grown on the hill).

3: **小牛上山吃草**
Little cow on hill eats grass (meaning the little cow goes up the hill to eat grass. Here 上, *on*, becomes a verb, *goes up*).

4: **小牛吃草上山**
Little cow eats grass on hill (meaning the little cow, to eat grass, goes up the hill).

5: **牛上山吃小草**
Cow on hill eats little grass (meaning the cow goes up the hill to eat a little grass).

6: **牛吃小山上草**
Cow eats little hill on grass (meaning the cow eats the grass on the little hill).

7: **牛小山上吃草**
Cow little hill on eats grass (meaning the cow is little and it eats grass on the hill).

8: **上山小牛吃草**

On hill little cow eats grass (meaning going up the hill, the little cow eats grass).

There are actually nine more combinations of these six characters, all resulting in different meanings. Most Chinese readers would understand the changes in meaning based on character order. This is one example of how flexible Chinese grammar is, and also an example of why it can be such a frustrating language to learn.

One aspect of Chinese that is easy for the English speaker to learn is the use of gender-based pronouns. Chinese has no gender forms other than she, he and it, which are written differently, but which all have the same pronunciation, 'ta'. This is an area where Chinese speakers learning English are challenged.

In addition, the different tenses of English verbs give Chinese speakers a big headache, as there are so many exceptions. They don't understand why it has to be I go, he goes, I went, I have gone, and so on.

Compared to Chinese sentences, English sentences can be very long. As long as the grammar is correct, a sentence can be used to express ideas, no matter how long and complicated it is. There are many modifiers one can use in English that help avoid confusion. In contrast, Chinese uses only short sentences to avoid misunderstandings.

English often employs the passive voice, as in the example, 'English is spoken by people all over the world.' This is never done in Chinese; instead, the sentence would be, 'People all over the world speak English'.

Even though English is technically a phonetic language, it is often necessary to read a word in order to understand how it sounds—a key feature in learning Chinese as well. In 1931, the linguist Zachrisson went as far as to say, 'English shares with Chinese the doubtful honor of being made up of chiefly ideographs, pictures of words which must be seen and remembered.' But his view was an extreme one and has not been shared by most linguists.

Another common feature is that both languages also have ridiculously large vocabularies, far greater than those of languages like French or Spanish.

And, as we have seen in this chapter, possibly the greatest shared feature is that both English and Chinese are challenging and require many years of learning to develop proficiency.

6

How Are Chinese Characters Created?

Most Western readers have an idea that each Chinese character (word) is actually a picture. This is only partially true. Over a period of more than four thousand years, the Chinese writing system has evolved from simple pictures (pictograms) into a complex system of over 50,000 characters. This can be difficult for people who are used to the phonetic system of writing to comprehend.

The Shang Dynasty (circa 1600–1100 BCE) is when the earliest system of Chinese character writing is believed to have formed. In the late 1890s, farmers in Xiaotun Village in the Anyang area of Henan province dug up thousands of animal bone and turtle shell pieces at the site of the ancient Shang capital city. They had markings on them; the Chinese people called them 'dragon bones', and they became popular as a type of medicine, ground to powder and sold for human consumption to treat various sorts of ailments.

In 1899, a scholar named Wang Yirong from the Beijing museum was doing research on the writing of the Zhou dynasty. *(Zhou dynasty—1046–256 BCE—came after the Shang dynasty. During the Zhou dynasty record keeping was much improved compared to the Shang dynasty and much is known about its writing.)* Wang noticed the dragon bones in an herbal shop and was intrigued by the markings on them. He recognized the connection between these markings and the ancient characters from the Zhou dynasty that he had been studying.

Wang Yirong's subsequent research revealed that the dragon bone pieces originated from the Shang period, around 1200 BCE. He noted that the markings were a developed system of writing. He called the bones and shells the 'Oracle Bones' and the script 'Oracle Bone Script'. The Oracle Bone Script was characterized by square and sharp lines that somewhat resembled objects.

Close up of the writings on an Oracle Bone

Markings on a turtle shell

During the Shang Dynasty, the bones and shells were used in divination ceremonies. Before important events (a battle, for example), diviners would carve out characters representing the possible outcomes. The shells or bones would then be heated over a fire and the cracks that formed on the pieces would be interpreted by the diviners. This practice was later abandoned and the bones and shells were forgotten.

In 1988, archeologists recovered animal bones and potsherds with markings on them in Damaidi in Ningxia, near Shaanxi in northwestern China. Among the markings on these bones and potsherds were about 2,000 symbols that looked like the markings on the Oracle Bones. The bones and potsherds were dated to around 7,000 to 8,000 years ago. If these markings prove to be writings, it is likely that the invention of Chinese characters began over 3,000 years earlier than the Shang period.

The Oracle Bone Script evolved to the Bronze Script, so called because the characters were inscriptions on bronze bells and tripod cauldrons. A large number of these artifacts have been recovered from the Shang and Zhou dynasties. The characters in this writing style are more remote (i.e., moving away from the original drawings of objects) from the primitive pictographs of the Oracle Bone Script. They are more regular and consistent, i.e., more like writing.

The next period of evolution in Chinese characters was the Seal Script (Big Seal and Small Seal), which came during the Warring States Period (475–221 BCE). Between the two subcategories, the Small Seal Script had greater influence and is sometimes simply referred to as the Seal Script. As you can see from the drawings below, they are even further away from the pictograms, and more like present-day Chinese characters.

When China was unified under the First Emperor, Qin Shihuang, in 221 BCE, which marked the beginning of the Qin Dynasty, the books and writings of the six defeated states were burnt and banned, and the writing in China became uniform. It was called the Official Script. It remained in use for centuries and is highly legible to modern readers. It has a rectilinear structure, which is similar to the modern standard script.

The Standard Script (also called Regular Script) matured stylistically during the Tang Dynasty (618–907 CE) and is still the most commonly used script in modern writings and publications. It looks taller than the preceding Official Script and is said to be easier and faster to write.

Below are drawings that illustrate the gradual evolution of the character for *horse*.

馬 = horse

(1) (2) (3) (4) (5) (6)

From left to right:

1) Oracle Bone Script (1600–1100 BCE)
2) Bronze Script (1046–256 BCE)
3) Big Seal Script (457–221 BCE)
4) Small Seal Script (457–221 BCE)
5) Official Script (221 BCE–618 CE)
6) Standard Script/Regular Script (618 CE onwards)

When people in ancient China began to write, they already had a developed spoken language. Like the Sumerians before them, the Chinese chose the most obvious representations: pictograms, which were slightly stylized versions of real-world objects.

Here are some examples of Chinese pictograms:

日 sun	水 water	女 woman
月 moon	雨 rain	人 man
目 eye	木 tree	母 mother
田 field	山 mountain	馬 horse

Once the Chinese started using pictograms, it quickly became apparent that they couldn't have a picture for every single word they wanted to say. How do you draw numbers? How do you say *bright* with a pictogram? How would you draw *danger*? What about *today*, *yesterday* and *tomorrow*? These are common words, but not easy ones to express in a simple pictogram.

These concepts already existed in the spoken language, so ideograms were developed to represent them.

Here are some examples of ideograms:

一 one	上 above	力 strength
二 two	下 below	凸 convex
三 three	中 middle	凹 concave

The Sumerians learned the limitations of the pictogram or ideogram system and invented the phonetic system, which is now the source of writing for all languages except Chinese. Even Japanese and Korean, which have adopted some Chinese characters into their written languages, are phonetically based and can be learned like most other languages: with sounds corresponding to characters. Once the rules of the alphabet are understood, it is possible to write the spoken language.

The Chinese, however, maintained the ancient system of symbols, and as the written language evolved, more complex symbols were devised. Some characters seem whimsical and may even be a result of their creator having fun; but for the most part, Chinese characters were created using symbolic representations of objects or ideas.

These characters were created throughout China's long history and by many people. Their development was complicated by the fact that characters were created by writers living in different historical periods, and in different parts of the country. This meant variations in sounds across several dialects over the years, which inevitably shaped the choice of some elements in the creation of new characters. Unlike French and Spanish, which were regulated only by prominent scholars, practically anyone could create Chinese characters. There were never any fixed rules the Chinese could draw upon when creating them. If they proved useful, they were adopted; otherwise, they would fade into obscurity through lack of use. A high school graduate in China probably recognizes about 4,000 characters, and to be scholastically fluent requires around 10,000. With approximately 50,000 Chinese characters in existence, this means that 40,000 of the known characters are rarely if ever used and have been essentially forgotten.

The art of creating Chinese characters is not completely without parameters, however. There are three elements to a Chinese character: image (form, the writing), sound, and meaning.

Traditionally, they are divided into six categories, or more precisely into the six principles of character formation. This classification is generally believed to have been devised by a scholar named Xu Shen in the second century in a dictionary called *Shuowen Jiezi* that he compiled during the Han Dynasty. While not the first dictionary in existence for the Chinese language, it was the first to analyze the structure of characters and to organize them by shared characteristics.

The first category of character formation is the pictogram or pictograph, which we've seen examples of above. This is the oldest form of character—images representing objects. During the past 4,000 years, they have been stylized and simplified, and some have lost their pictographic flavor. Contrary to popular belief, pictograms make up only a small portion (about 600, or 4%) of Chinese characters.

The second category is the ideogram, which as we've seen is used to express an abstract idea through iconic form, including iconic modification of pictographic characters. For example, the pictogram for tree (木) has been modified to represent other words here:

本 This is *root*—a tree with the base indicated by an extra stroke.

末 This is *apex*—the reverse of *root* (本) with an extra stroke on top.

The third category includes compound pictograms and compound ideograms. These characters are formed by combining one or more pictograms or ideograms. Each part contributes to the meaning of the new compound character. They comprise about 13% of Chinese characters.

Here are some examples:

好 good (woman + child)	雷 thunder (rain cloud over a field)
安 peaceful (woman under a roof)	明 bright (sun + moon)
家 home/family (pig under a roof)	林 forest (two trees)
男 man/male (field + strength)	森 jungle (three trees)
思 thought (heart + field)	休 rest (man leaning against a tree)

As you can see, some compound characters seem to follow logic, while others defy it. American poet Ezra Pound had a theory on how the character for *East* (東) was invented. He speculated that 東 was essentially a superposition of the characters for *tree* (木) and *sun* (日). He saw the character as a picture of the sun enmeshed in a tree's branches, suggesting a sunrise, which occurs in the east. This of course was his own opinion; we have no idea what the inventor had in mind when the character was created over 4,000 years ago. Pound's guess is a reasonable one—it very likely did have something to do with the sun rising. But when a Chinese person looks at the character 東 (*East*), he or she does not see a sunrise, but rather sees the character as its own entity instead of breaking out its component parts.

The fourth principle of character formation is a little more complex. This category represents about 80% of all existing characters, due to the extremely productive use of this technique to extend the Chinese vocabulary. This method is still used to form new characters.

The category comprises the semantic-phonetic compounds. These characters consist of two parts: a semantic component (called a radical), which hints at the meaning of the character, and a phonetic component that gives a clue to the pronunciation of the character.

The semantic component only gives a broad hint of the meaning, a general indicator of the area of knowledge referred to, such as 'human affairs', 'water-related', 'botany', 'manual actions', or 'emotions'. Unless the word is already known, the meaning cannot usually be guessed purely by looking at the character. These are just hints and not always dependable.

Some of the semantic radicals are:

水 water	子 child	木 tree
口 mouth	山 mountain	言 speech

Phonetic components are generally a more reliable indication of pronunciation than semantic components are of meaning—i.e., the phonetic components help more to understand how the character should *sound* than the semantic components help with the character's *meaning*.

Tone is a major feature of the Chinese language, and is a difficult concept for non-Chinese to grasp because it has no parallel in the English language. For example, there may be two Chinese words that are spoken with the same sound—and to untrained ears, sound identical—but if the word is spoken with a high rising tone it means one thing, while spoken with a low dipping tone it means another thing altogether.

There are four tones, plus a neutral (or no) tone that can affect how a character sounds (and, thus, what it means). When we express these tones in English, we use accents to indicate the different tones. This was discussed in the chapter on Pinyin, but for reference here, the four tones again are:

ˉ	ˊ	ˇ	ˋ
Tone 1	Tone 2	Tone 3	Tone 4
High level	High rising	Low dipping	High falling

Here are some examples of characters in this category, where the semantic component (meaning) isn't always helpful, but the phonetic component helps to indicate the sound. They are all pronounced 'gu' and may be the same tone or a different tone, based on the radical of 古 or gǔ.

古 pronounced gǔ (with the third tone) and means *ancient.* This is the phonetic radical.

估 adding the radical 'person', also pronounced gǔ (third tone) and means *to guess.*

詁 adding the radical 'words', also pronounced gǔ (third tone) and means *commentaries.*

鈷 adding the radical 'metal', pronounced gū (first tone) and means *cobalt.*

蛄 adding the radical 'insect', pronounced gū (first tone) and refers to a specific type of insect.

姑 adding the radical 'female', the word is pronounced gú (second tone) and means *aunt.*

The previous examples all use phonetic components such that all the characters have the same pronunciations with perhaps different tones. The following examples use the semantic radical of water, 水 (sui), which is simplified to three dots. They appear on the left side of each character. The phonetic component is on the right side. In these examples, the pronunciation of the character is quite different in each case, because the common element in each is semantic (again, related to meaning), and the phonetic element in each is different.

河 = river, pronounced he. The phonetic component is 可 (pronounced ke), which means *approve.* The pronunciation of river (he) is different from the phonetic component of ke.

湖 = lake, pronounced hu. The phonetic component is 胡 (pronounced hu), which is a family name and has no real meaning, and the final character is pronounced the same as the phonetic component.

沖 = riptide or flush, pronounced chong. The phonetic component 中 (pronounced zhong) means *middle.* The final character is pronounced chong and has diverged from that of its phonetic indicator of zhong.

滑 = slippery, pronounced hua. The phonetic component 骨 (pronounced gu) means *bone.* In this case, the pronunciation of the final character is quite different from the phonetic component. It is interesting to speculate how this word was invented. Perhaps the inventor made a connection between slipping on water and broken bones; only he knew what was in his mind when it was created. The pronunciation of the original character could have changed over the course of several thousand years.

As you can see, there are no real rules as to what form (character) goes with a specific sound. Although some rules seem to fit with many characters, often they simply do not apply, or it is impossible to apply them because of the nature of the non-phonetic writing. This is why learning Chinese can be so overwhelming: there's no escaping the memorization work.

The fifth category of character formation is 'Rebus' or 'Borrowed', which is also called borrowings or phonetic loan characters. This category covers cases where an existing character is used to represent an unrelated word with a similar pronunciation.

來 This character, pronounced lai, depicts the wheat plant and meant *wheat* in ancient times. It was a pictogram. Because the words for 'wheat' and the verb 'to come' were pronounced the same, the character 來 was then borrowed to signify *to come*.

麥 The pronunciation of the original word meaning *wheat* has changed in modern times to mai (now written as shown), and the original homophony between the two characters has disappeared.

自 pronounced zi used to mean 'nose' but now it exclusively means *oneself*.

萬 pronounced wan originally meant 'scorpion' but now it means *ten thousand.*

There are very few characters that belong to this group.

The sixth category is Transformed Cognate or Derived characters. Characters in this category did not represent the same meaning but have bifurcated through other semantic drifts. There are very few characters in this category.

Example: Both of these characters used to mean *an elderly person*. But now:

老 pronounced lao, means *old*
考 pronounced kao, means *examination*

The composition of a character can sometimes seem arbitrary, because its meaning was determined by the inventor of that character, and there were many inventors of many characters throughout China's long history. Just as with alphabet-based languages, which evolve over time, new words representing new ideas emerge; but for Chinese, the characters themselves will continue to evolve as the language and ideas grow and change.

The Chinese writing system is truly unique and how it works is drastically different from an alphabet system. It may take some effort to fully understand how it works, but knowing a little more about it is helpful in understanding other aspects of Chinese culture, history, philosophy, customs, psyche and so on. This may open up another world for you and may even entice you to study the language!

7

How Do You Sound Out an Unknown Character?

You can use this chapter as an exercise to test your brain to see if you can detect the subtle differences between the Chinese characters, as in the 'spot the difference' game!

A phonemic orthography is an orthography (system for writing a language) in which the graphemes (written symbols) correspond to the phonemes (spoken sounds). Languages don't usually have perfectly phonemic orthographies—i.e., the written characters do not always correspond to the sounds of the words. We find this often in the English language, which is highly non-phonemic. Italian and Spanish are much more phonemic, meaning the spelling of a word frequently corresponds to its sound.

In English, the word 'dog' corresponds with the letters D-O-G. Once an English speaker learns the rules of the alphabet, he or she can make the sounds that correspond with the letters to say the word. Similarly, in Spanish, the word for dog is 'perro'. The speaker can pronounce the word by sounding it out according to the rules of that alphabet.

But Chinese has no alphabet—no phonemic orthography. The writing that goes with the sound does not follow rules like that of an alphabet; instead, each word (i.e., character) that represents an object or idea has to be learnt and memorized.

For example, *dog* is pronounced 'gou' in Mandarin and the word to represent gou is 狗. There is no way for a reader to see the character 狗 and know how it should be pronounced unless having been taught to do so.

In spite the language being non-alphabetical, the sounds of many Chinese characters can be predicted. Some linguists even claim that Chinese is, in its own way, phonetic to a certain extent.

How do the Chinese read aloud characters that they haven't seen before? How does one guess the pronunciation of unknown characters? Unlike an alphabet-based language like Spanish or English, where does one even begin to guess at a character's sound? The Pinyin system solved the problem of what sound goes with what character, but what if you are just looking at the character, without any Pinyin notation?

When attempting to pronounce an unfamiliar character, the first thing one needs to do is to analyze it. As discussed in the previous chapter, over 80% of all Chinese characters are created by the 'semantic-phonetic compound' method. These characters consist of two parts: a semantic component or radical, which hints at the meaning of the character, and a phonetic component that gives a clue to the pronunciation of the character.

Characters containing the same phonetic component may have:

1. the same sound and the same tone,
2. the same sound but a different tone,
3. the same initial or final sound, or
4. a different sound and a different tone.

The truth is that understanding this system is not often helpful in figuring out the pronunciation of a character, but it is better than nothing.

There is a Chinese saying about trying to sound out a new character: *If there is a side, read the side. If there is no side, read the middle. If there is no middle, just guess.*

The best way to sound out an unknown character is to learn as many common phonetic components as possible. The following are examples of the four types of semantic-phonetic compounds:

1) All the characters have the same sound (syllable) and the same tone.

The following compounds contain this phonetic component, meaning *emperor*: 皇. They are all pronounced huáng, and are all spoken with the second tone (high rising). This part of the character is usually on the right. Depending on the final character that it becomes part of, huáng 皇 may be slightly different in its appearance, such as in size, width, or height; but it always has the identical strokes. This is because each character has to fit into a square of the same size, no matter how complex or simple the character is.

The semantic component (that gives a clue to the meaning) is usually on the left of the character, but sometimes it can be on the top, below, or around—i.e., enclosing the phonetic component, such as in the last example below.

Again, these characters are all pronounced huáng, with the same high rising tone.

惶 *afraid* with radical 'heart'

煌 *brilliant* with radical 'fire'

蝗 *locust* with radical 'insect'

隍 *moat* with radical 'mound'

鰉 *sturgeon* with radical 'fish'

遑 *hasten* with radical 'run'

凰 *female phoenix* with radical 'bench'

2) The characters may have the same syllable but a different tone in some cases.

馬 mǎ, (*horse*) is the phonetic component found in the following characters. It is pronounced with the third tone, which is low dipping.

瑪 mǎ, *agate* with the radical 'jade', pronounced at the third tone.

碼 mǎ, *weights* with radical 'stone', pronounced at the third tone.

嗎 ma, *question particle* with radical 'mouth', pronounced with no tone.

媽 mā, *mother* with the radical 'female', pronounced at the first tone, high level.

螞 mǎ, *ant* with radical 'insect', pronounced at the third tone.

鎷 mǎ, *masurium* with radical 'metal', pronounced at the third tone.

榪 mà, *clamp* with radical 'tree', pronounced at the fourth tone, high falling.

罵 mà, *scold* with radical 'mouth', pronounced at the fourth tone.

3) The characters may have the same initial or final sound.

堯 yao is the phonetic component in these characters (you will notice below that the y changes to i after a consonant). It is a family name, after the name of an emperor, and has no real meaning otherwise.

僥 *lucky* with radical 'man', pronounced jiao.

澆 *sprinkle* with radical 'water', pronounced jiao.

磽 *stony soil* with radical 'stone', pronounced qiao.

翹 *tail feather* with radical 'feather', pronounced qiao.

曉 *dawn* with radical 'sun', pronounced xiao.

撓 *scratch* with radical 'hand', pronounced nao.

譊 *dispute* with radical 'word', pronounced nao.

橈 *oar* with radical 'wood', pronounced nao.

鐃 *hand-bells* with radical 'metal', pronounced nao.

嬈 *graceful* with radical 'female' pronounced nao.

繞 *wind around* with radical 'silk', pronounced rao.

蕘 *rushes* with radical 'grass', pronounced rao.

蟯 *tapeworm* with radical 'insect', pronounced rao.

饒 *abundant* with radical 'food', pronounced rao.

燒 *burn* with radical 'fire', pronounced shao.

4) The characters may have a different sound and a different tone.

王 wang, meaning *king*, is the phonetic component in the following characters.

汪 *watery* with radical 'water', pronounced wang.

枉 *oppression* with radical 'tree', pronounced wang.

旺 *bright* with radical 'sun', pronounced wang.

弄 *toy with* with radical 'hands folded' below, pronounced nong.

聖 *sacred* with radicals 'ear' and 'mouth' above, pronounced sheng.

玉 *jade* by adding a dot to 王, pronounced yu.

By now, you have come across a number of semantic radicals such as *water*, *tree*, *sun*, *man*, *horse*, *word*, *female* and so on. A semantic radical really is of little help in determining the meaning of a character, as it only gives a broad hint. But it is better than no hint. In contrast, the phonetic components are much more useful in determining how the character should sound. If we know enough phonetic radicals, we have a good chance of knowing how to sound out Chinese characters.

By combining the large number of phonetic components with a large number of semantic radicals, you can see how so many characters can be created.

Chinese is a fascinating—and often frustrating—language. It sometimes seems to have developed beyond simple communication, as if inventing new characters has become a game of complexity and creativity.

It is simply beyond the capacity of the human brain to remember over 50,000 characters, and the sheer volume makes sounding them out just as difficult. In spite of the phonetic hints found in many of the characters' components, the utility of developing skill in recognizing them remains limited. Pinyin is the phonetic solution for non-Chinese speakers to make connections between the characters and sounds, but it is not a language; it is a tool for navigating around the challenging character system.

8

The Dialects: Why Chinese is Not One Language

When I was growing up, my family moved often and we lived in very different communities. I feel fortunate that I can speak fluently three of the major dialects (Hakka, Mandarin and Cantonese), I can get by with two (Min and Shanghainese) and I could probably express myself well enough to save my life with the other two (Gan and Xiang)!

The term *dialect* generally refers to mutually intelligible varieties of a single language, such as British English, American English, Australian English and so on. But distinction between dialects and languages often exists for political and sociological reasons rather than linguistic ones. Chinese people do accept that Chinese is a single language with a number of different dialects; but for the most part, these dialects are not mutually intelligible, which supports the linguistic argument that they should really be considered distinct languages.

As discussed previously, the written form of Chinese is perceived as being uniform throughout the country and is generally referred to as Hanyu, Han language or language of the Han people. The character 漢 or 汉 in the simplified form is used to refer to the Chinese people and comes from the Han Dynasty (206 BCE–220 CE).

The main written form of Chinese is based chiefly on the Mandarin spoken by educated people in the Beijing area. Each character represents both sound and meaning. Words in Chinese can be made up of one or more syllables and a single character represents each syllable.

Chinese belongs to the Sinitic or Chinese branch of the Sino-Tibetan language family. The present varieties of spoken Chinese all descended from Middle Chinese, which was spoken in China during the Southern and Northern Dynasties, and the Sui, Tang and Song Dynasties (5th–12th centuries CE). Old Chinese was spoken during the Shang and Zhou Dynasties and the Warring States Period (1600–256 BCE).

Most linguists generally agree that there are seven major Chinese dialect groups. They are:

- Mandarin, Putonghua or common speech: There are about 700 million native speakers in the north and southwest plus another 300 million non-native speakers.
- Wu or Shanghainese: Spoken by about 100 million people in the coastal area around Shanghai and Zhejiang.
- Yue or Cantonese: Spoken by about 70 million people in Guangdong, Guangxi and overseas communities.
- Min: Spoken by about 40 million people in Fujian and coastal areas of the south, Taiwan and Southeast Asia.
- Hakka: Spoken by at least 40 million people, and possibly as many as 80 million. Half of them are scattered between Guangdong, Guangxi, Fujian and Sichuan with the rest in Taiwan and overseas.
- Xiang: Spoken by about 46 million people in Hunan and surrounding areas.
- Gan: Spoken by about 23 million people, mostly in Jiangxi.

These seven dialects are mutually unintelligible.

Mandarin

The northern varieties of Chinese are generally known as the Mandarin dialects. These dialects are spoken by more than two-thirds of Chinese people, covering an area more than three-fourths of the country. It extends over all of north China and Sichuan, and parts of the northwest and southwest over terrains that are generally flat.

The Mandarin dialect can be subdivided into four groups:

1. Northern Mandarin, spoken in the northeast; includes the Beijing dialect.
2. Northwestern Mandarin, which includes dialects of the Loess plateau and areas to the west.
3. Southern Mandarin, spoken in Sichuan and adjacent areas.
4. Eastern or Lower Yangzi Mandarin, spoken around the Nanjing area.

These dialects can be very diverse. Deng Xiaoping, leader of the People's Republic of China from the late 1970s until his death in 1997, came from Sichuan and spoke a sub-dialect of Mandarin. Even though Sichuanese is considered a branch of the Mandarin dialect, I could barely understand his speech that was supposedly given in his version of Mandarin. When I worked in the Guilin area off and on for several years, I had to listen very carefully to understand the language. The people in this area speak a dialect that is also considered a branch of Mandarin, but the intonation is quite different compared to the standard Mandarin.

Wu or Shanghainese

'Shanghainese' often refers to all Wu dialects and is a dialect of Northern Wu. The Wu dialects are spoken in the Yangzi River Delta region and the coastal region around Shanghai. Shanghai is often referred to as the New York of China and its cultural impact on the rest of the country has long been considerable, especially during the years before WWII when Shanghai was an international city known as the Paris of Asia. The Shanghainese people are regarded as sophisticated and trend-setting.

Shanghainese is rich in vowels (twelve of which are phonemic) and in consonants. Its tonal system is quite different from other Chinese dialects. Shanghainese has two level tonal contrasts only (high and low: for example, má and mà), unlike Mandarin and Cantonese, which are typical contour tonal languages (containing multiple tones: for example, the four tones of mā, má, mǎ, and mà in Mandarin).

Shanghai did not become a major commerce center until it was opened to foreign investment during the late Qing dynasty, after which its dialect became the *lingua franca* of the region. In 1949, the government imposed Mandarin as the national language for all of China and the influence of Shanghainese began to diminish. Shanghai has now become home to a large number of migrants from all over the country and Mandarin is the most commonly spoken dialect.

The Shanghainese pronunciation is unintelligible to standard Mandarin speakers. To the Cantonese, it may as well be a foreign language.

Yue or Cantonese

Yue is spoken in much of Guangdong province. It is an old language going back to the kingdom of Yue and is thought to be the language of the Tang Dynasty.

Cantonese is a popular dialect since it is spoken in Hong Kong and much of Southeast Asia, and in Chinatowns in North America and Australia where early immigrants came mostly from the Canton area. It is one of the most difficult dialects to learn because of its many tones. In addition, Cantonese has some of its own written characters, which are not found in the standard Mandarin dictionary.

The status of Cantonese in southern China is an emotional issue. Even though Hong Kong returned to Chinese rule in 1997, many people there can neither speak nor understand Mandarin, and they continue using only Cantonese. In 2010, when the government planned to switch some television programs to Mandarin, there were widespread protests, and the government ultimately abandoned the idea.

Even someone like me, who grew up in Hong Kong and speaks Cantonese with no accent, can still feel like an outsider. My family didn't speak Cantonese at home, so in spite of my fluency, I was unfamiliar with some of the Cantonese colloquial expressions and words.

The Yue refer to themselves as people of the Tang (Dynasty), calling their country Tang Mountain, their clothing Tang clothes, their cuisine Tang food.

It is said that a Tang poem read in Cantonese keeps more of its original patterns of rhyme than when it is read in Mandarin, because it has undergone the least amount of transformation and has preserved its sound system with the greatest fidelity. This is one of the reasons Yue is thought to be the language spoken during the Tang Dynasty rather than Mandarin.

Cantonese is a lively and descriptive language. Later in this book, there will be a chapter on Hong Kong Cantonese.

Min

South Min is spoken in Fujian province, at the northeastern tip of Guangdong and in Taiwan. Northern Min is spoken in Fuzhou, Shouning and other areas. The dialects of Xiamen, Shantou and Fuzhou are the best-known Min dialects. There are huge differences within the Min dialects in terms of tones and even syntax.

Min can also be heard in areas outside of these primary dialect regions because the people are seafarers and fishermen. Many Min have settled along the coastal areas of Guangdong and the periphery of Hainan Island. The dialect is also spoken throughout Southeast Asia.

Fujian province is relatively isolated from the interior of China. It is mountainous with few navigable rivers. It was the last part of the country to be settled by Chinese people. This geographic isolation has kept the Min dialects out of the Chinese linguistic mainstream, leaving them with some very archaic features not seen in other dialects, such as a greater number of monosyllabic words. Because of the isolation between various Min populations, there are at least nine mutually unintelligible dialects within this group.

Hakka

The Hakka are scattered throughout most of south China. Hakka villages can be found in the countryside from Sichuan to Taiwan and the hillier parts of Guangdong, Guangxi and southern Fujian, as well as parts of Southeast Asia.

Meixian (Plum County) in the mountainous northeastern region of Guangdong is considered the homeland of the Hakka. Hakka literally means *guest people*. It is a name given to them by the Cantonese as they migrated into Cantonese-speaking areas in the south. Until recently, many Cantonese and Min mistakenly thought that the Hakka were not Chinese at all but some kind of non-Han minority.

The Hakka identify themselves as Northern Chinese. Genealogies and historical records indicate that many of the ancestors of the Hakka were originally from the northern plains.

The majority of Hakka dialects have six tones, while some have less. Among these dialects, there can be vast differences in tones and even syntax, and some may even be mutually unintelligible, especially comparing the Hakka dialects in Guangdong and Sichuan. These two groups of Hakka people have been separated for a long time, and their dialects have evolved in very different ways. Surrounding Meixian are the counties of Pingyuan, Dabu, Jiaoling, Xingning, Wuhua and Fengshun, all of which have different versions of the Hakka dialect. Each is said to have its own special phonological features. Other Hakka dialects include Lufeng, Huizhou, Longyan, Changtin and others outside of the main Hakka area around Meixian. In Taiwan, there are two main Hakka dialects: Sixian and Haifeng.

Hakka and Cantonese (Yue) are believed to be the languages used during the Tang dynasty. It is a language far older than standard Mandarin.

Xiang (also known as Hunanese)

The Xiang dialect is spoken in Hunan and is divided into New Xiang and Old Xiang. New Xiang is spoken in the northwestern part of Hunan as well as in larger towns and cities. Old Xiang is the form of Chinese generally heard in mountain and farming areas. These two forms of the dialect are quite different and communication between the two is very difficult. New Xiang has been influenced by Southwestern Mandarin, and speakers of these two dialects would be able to communicate with each other.

Xiang is spoken by over 36 million people in China, mainly in Hunan province and the surrounding areas, as well as in several places in Guizhou and Guangdong provinces.

The most famous Xiang speaker was Mao Zedong, whose speech was totally unintelligible to me on television, even though he thought he was speaking Mandarin! Xiang is notoriously difficult for the rest of China to understand.

Gan

These little-known and little-studied varieties of Chinese are spoken mostly in Jiangxi province, which stretches from the hills and mountain passes along the border of Guangdong province northward to the Yangzi River. Some Gan dialects are also spoken in the eastern part of Hunan, and some parts of Hubei province as well. The Gan dialect area is not clearly differentiated from the dialect areas adjacent to it.

As you can see, Chinese is not just one language. Even within the individual dialects, regional differences can make them unintelligible to one another. Given the disparity in the dialects, it is truly amazing that Chinese people who otherwise cannot understand each other in speech can understand each other in writing. This is the reason why, in spite of the written language being difficult to learn (even for the natives), the Chinese have not found a substitute. It enables people with such different spoken languages to communicate with each other in written form.

9

Can Chinese be Alphabetized?

The more correct question is: *Can Mandarin be alphabetized?* The answer is yes.

Most linguists agree that Chinese is not one language, but rather a group or branch of related languages that have less in common than the Romance languages have with each other. Mandarin is spoken mainly in the north. There are six or seven other major languages spoken in the rest of the country and abroad. Among them, Cantonese, Shanghainese and Min are the most prominent. These southern varieties are primary languages for tens of millions of Chinese speakers. It is estimated that there are 100 million Shanghainese and 60 million Cantonese speakers worldwide. Each has significant differences in vocabulary, phonology, and even syntax, and all are mutually unintelligible.

Since the non-Mandarin varieties of Chinese are mostly unwritten, they are often not portrayed as full-fledged languages, even though they qualify as languages by any linguistic measure.

Learning the Pinyin method of Mandarin for a non-Mandarin speaker is like learning a second language, just as Indians have to learn English or Hindi in addition to their own language.

If the other Chinese dialects became Romanized, China would indeed become like Europe, with the added complication that a Mandarin speaker reading Romanized Cantonese wouldn't have the faintest idea what it meant, whereas an Italian reading Spanish could more or less get the gist of the text.

The following are examples of phrases in Mandarin and Cantonese of 'I like to eat Chinese food':

Mandarin: wo xi huan chi zhong guo cai

Cantonese: ngoh jung yi sihk tohng chaan

One can see that Cantonese may as well be Greek to the Mandarin speaker, and vice versa.

China is much like Western Europe was before each country had their respective written languages. Prior to that, the Romance languages were spoken, but Latin was the common written language. As the speech became more and more different, countries like Portugal, Spain, Italy, France and Romania developed their own written language as well.

Before the First Emperor unified China, it was divided into different kingdoms, each speaking its own language with its own form of writing. After Emperor Qin defeated the diverse civilizations, he burned all the books in their languages, leaving only the Qin Kingdom's written language. The result is what we know as China today. Several regions (old kingdoms) continued to use their spoken languages, which evolved into unique dialects, while still keeping the same written language. Having the same written characters gives the illusion that China has one language, even though the same character has a different sound (syllable) in each dialect. The common view among linguists is that Chinese is actually a group of languages, such as Cantonese or Yue, which was spoken in the kingdom of Yue, and the Wu (Shanghainese), which was spoken in the kingdom of Wu.

Mandarin or Putonghua (the common speech) certainly can be and is being alphabetized with Pinyin. The problem is that the people in China who don't speak Mandarin have no idea how to read the Pinyin in Mandarin. As I mentioned earlier, Mandarin is a dialect spoken around Beijing. Even under the

Mandarin dialect, there are sub-dialects in areas away from Beijing. As mentioned earlier, Deng Xiaoping spoke a Sichuanese dialect, and as a standard Mandarin speaker myself, I had no idea what he was saying when I used to watch him speak on TV. If Mandarin is alphabetized, I wonder if speakers of non-standard dialects such as Xi'an, Sichuan and Guangxi would be able to understand and read standard Mandarin in Pinyin, thus further complicating attempts to Romanize the 'Chinese language'.

The Chinese have used the character system since 1200 BCE. They originally regarded themselves as the center of the universe, calling their country Middle Kingdom, and believing that the character form of writing was uniquely suited to their culture. Because of its isolation from other countries, China was probably never exposed to the alphabet form of writing until a few hundred years ago. It was only about a hundred years ago, when it became obvious that China, once a pioneer in science and discoveries, was far behind Western countries with alphabetic writing systems, that they began thinking about switching their system to a phonetic one.

One obvious obstacle to switching to an alphabet system is the presence of thousands of homonyms—characters with the same sound but totally different meanings. There are a limited number of sounds in Chinese, approximately 1,600 syllables that include the tones and about 400 if tones are excluded. (English has over 8,000 syllables.) There are as many as 50,000 Chinese characters. With so few sounds, one can see that many characters have to share the same sound. For example, the *Mathews Chinese-English Dictionary* lists 90 characters for the single syllable 'li'. In such a case, the reader may not know which characters the writer has in mind. In fact, many scholars who were opposed to the idea of Romanization gave examples such as the following to demonstrate that alphabetization would not work:

西溪犀 喜嬉戲 Xi xi xi, xi xi xi
稀熙夕 携犀戲 Xi xi xi, xi xi xi
稀熙細 習洗犀 Xi xi xi, xi xi xi
犀吸溪 戲襲熙 Xi xi xi, xi xi xi
稀熙嘻 希息戲 Xi xi xi, xi xi xi
惜犀唏 喜襲熙 Xi xi xi, xi xi xi

The passage translates as follows:

West Creek rhinoceros enjoys romping and playing.
Xi (family name) Xi (given name) takes rhinoceros to play every evening.
Xi Xi meticulously practices washing rhinoceros.
Rhinoceros sucks creek, playfully attacks Xi.
Xi Xi laughing hopes to stop playing.
Too bad rhinoceros neighing enjoys attacking Xi.

The above passages are written in classical Chinese and are incapable of being Pinyinized. When the passages are transcribed alphabetically, they make no sense to the ear at all.

Another scholar tried to outdo the author of the previous example by writing an even longer passage to prove the point about too many homonyms:

Shi shi shi shi shi
施氏食獅史

Shi shi shi shi shi shi, shi shi shi shi. Shi shi shi shi shi shi shi shi.

石室詩士施氏，嗜食獅，誓食十獅。氏時時遂市视獅。

Shi shi, shi shi shi, shi shi shi shi shi, shi shi, shi shi shi shi shi,
十時，氏適市，適十獅逞市。是時，氏视是十獅，

Shi shi shi shi shi, shi shi shi shi shi shi, shi shi shi shi shi shi shi shi,
侍十石矢誓，是侍石獅逝世。氏拾是十獅尸适石室，

Shi shi shi, shi shi shi shi shi shi, shi shi shi, shi shi shi shi shi shi shi,
石室濕，仕侍試栻石室，石室栻，氏始試食是十獅尸，

Shi shi, shi shi shi shi shi.
是時，氏始識事 是事實。

Shi shi shi shi!
試釋是事！

His was a nonsensical but intelligible story about a poet called Gentleman Shi who lived in a stone house and became addicted to eating lions. He went to search for them and found ten in a market, but noticed that they were all dead when he arrived home, and so on.

As you can see, transcribed into phonetics, every character would be 'shi'. The last four characters say, 'Go ahead and check, this is true!' Many more passages could easily be constructed like the two examples above. But these are extreme illustrations written in classical Chinese. Many people feel that these two scholars were being dramatic and were playing games with a form of artificial writing (classical Chinese) that has long been obsolete and has no bearing on current problems with writing Chinese. Writings done in a style close to actual speech should be adaptable to alphabetic writing.

In doing research for this chapter, I came across the following passage posted on the Internet:

Ruguo Zhongguoren dou yong Luomazi xie Hanyu, yiding biancheng shijie biaozhun yuyan! Ni yijing dong le ba?

Without difficulty I was able to read it as, 'If all Chinese people use the Romanization to write Chinese, it would certainly become the standard language of the world! Do you already understand that?'

Mandarin can definitely be alphabetized. Take for example the character 想 with the syllable of 'xiang', which most Mandarin speakers would recognize right away as *think*. If Mandarin were Romanized, and we looked at 'xiang' enough times, we would eventually learn to associate it with *think* in the right context. Like any language, it is just a matter of being exposed to it enough times.

If Vietnamese could be Romanized, Mandarin, which has fewer tones, certainly can be as well; but it would take political will and time. Prior to the Romanization of the Vietnamese language, few could read or write, as the official written language Quoc Ngu was adopted from modified Chinese characters. Except for government officials, the very wealthy and scholars, the masses could not afford to learn to read or write because of the time and effort it would take. The process of Romanization took more than one generation, but now it seems to work well. The advantage for Vietnam is that it only had one spoken language to begin with. There are dialects, but they are mutually intelligible and political unity was never a factor.

In addition, there wasn't much Vietnamese literature written in the form of characters, and most people couldn't read it anyway. Add to this the fact that Quoc Ngu is not a native language, and we can see that cultural continuity was not an issue either.

On the other hand, Japanese would also be a good candidate for Romanization, but it has not made a complete transition as Vietnamese has. It would actually work better than Vietnamese or Mandarin because it is a non-tonal language. Even though the Japanese have long used the Romaji (Romanization) of the Japanese language and it is very successful for helping foreigners learn, it nevertheless has not replaced the Kanji (the adopted Chinese characters), which they still depend on a great deal. Even though Kanji is of foreign origin, the Japanese have used it for over a thousand years. So far, they haven't given it up to depend entirely on their phonetic Romaji system. Converting Japanese into the Latin alphabet would be more straightforward and less ambiguous than converting Mandarin, because of Mandarin's tones and countless homonyms.

There is no problem with political unity in Japan as there is just one language, and even though there are regional dialects, all of them are mutually intelligible.

Perhaps the Japanese decided not to alphabetize their language for cultural reasons. They have literature, poetry, calligraphy and paintings that use Kanji. These would be lost if they only relied on Romaji. If the Japanese have not done it after all these years, I doubt China would make the switch for some of the same reasons. If anything, perhaps the Chinese would utilize both systems to complement each other as the Japanese have done.

Political unity is a big reason why China wouldn't want to completely Romanize its language. The government wants the Chinese people to continue to believe that they are united under one language. If Romanization occurs, the Shanghainese and Cantonese would be constantly reminded that they really have little in common with the Northerners who speak other dialects and eat wheat instead of rice. If it were not for the common writing system, there would be no way for the different regions to communicate with each other, unless everyone in China was required to learn standard Mandarin.

There is no way that the Cantonese would give up their ages-old dialect to speak Mandarin. The Chinese spoken in Singapore is made up of several major dialects. Students are encouraged to speak Mandarin at home, but after several decades, people still speak their dialect at home and only use Mandarin in school or other public situations.

If China were to go with Romanization as many scholars suggest, they wouldn't have to give up the characters. Anyone who wanted to study the characters and read original texts still could on their own time, just as the English who wish to study old texts such as the Bible, Shakespeare's plays or Chaucer would take special lessons to learn to read and comprehend them. Most modern Greeks cannot read classical Greek, which they leave to the study of scholars. Perhaps China could do the same. It certainly is not true that if Chinese were alphabetized, all of China's past literature would have to be translated into Pinyin.

Chinese characters have probably never been a major factor in preserving the unity of China. In reality, it was political unity that prevented linguistic disunity, and historically only the gentry (a very small percentage of the population) was united by its knowledge of the characters.

Preserving the characters for those who want to study them while adding an independent Pinyin for general use as an aid in China's modernization may be the solution to making it easier for the masses to read and write. In Vietnam, prior to Romanization, most people could not read or write. Since the reform, those who could not read Vietnamese literature in the Nom (adopted Chinese characters) originally, can now read them in translation in the alphabet-based script.

India is a good example of a country with many languages that still remains united. English or Hindi are the common languages that bind them. Since its independence, there has never been any danger of India unraveling because of the different languages. *If anything, it would be the different religions that could cause divides in the country.*

The argument in favor of language reform is that the present system of characters is not serving the Chinese people well. Ongoing attempts to simplify the characters do not solve the basic problem. The masses may spend less time writing the characters with reduced strokes, but they still have to memorize each character. In some cases, the simplification is so ridiculous that the modified form bears no resemblance to the traditional form, such as the unrecognizable characters for the Hong Kong and Shanghai Bank mentioned earlier. Simplification may not be achieving what the government had in mind; instead, it creates the opposite effect of making the language more difficult to learn, since many simplified characters do not follow any rules. This effectively creates two systems of writing, complicating things for people inside and outside China who study the language, and further widening the cultural and language gap between China and Hong Kong, Taiwan and much of Southeast Asia's Chinese community. In fact, there is now a movement in

China to return the simplified characters to their traditional forms.

With rapid global developments in science and technology, China needs an alphabet-based language if it wants to keep up. The solution may be to keep the two systems—the character and Pinyin—side by side, somewhat like the Japanese system of mixed texts, which uses both Chinese characters and their version of phonetics at the same time. But this still does not solve the problem of the many dialects spoken in China. For the Pinyin writing system to work, every Chinese would need to speak standard Mandarin, which wouldn't be an easy task to accomplish and would essentially make many of them bilingual.

Whatever the future of the Chinese language, its issues will not be easily solved. Chinese writing, especially as expressed in calligraphy, is itself part of Chinese culture, and most Chinese are reluctant to give it up entirely.

Perhaps no decision needs to be made, and scholars involved in current debates should just let the evolution of the language occur. When more and more people know less and less about the character writing system (Chapter 17 is *Amnesia and the Chinese Language*), people will simply vote with their hands and forget about the characters, using the Pinyin system more and more, letting the character writing system die a natural death.

10

Is the Chinese Language Monosyllabic?

It would be difficult to have a functional language with about 400 syllables, multiplied to about 1,600 with tones. With the number of objects and ideas that we have to express in a language, it is simply impossible for a language to be monosyllabic.

Chinese words are not monosyllabic, but the characters are. A character is not a word. According to *Webster's New World Dictionary*, a word is 'a speech sound or series of such sounds, having meaning as a unit of language' and 'the written or printed representation of this'.

It is true that many Chinese words do have only one syllable. This unfortunately makes for a lot of homonyms, which can be confusing in speech. Classical and Middle Chinese are often considered monosyllabic languages, at least in the written form. Many scholars feel that Classical Chinese was written in such a terse manner (like a telegram) because of the scarcity of writing material. I cannot imagine people spoke the way Classical Chinese was written, as there would be so much room for misunderstanding because of the homonyms. Modern Chinese is polysyllabic.

The Chinese writing system is the main reason that spoken Chinese is often mistakenly described as monosyllabic. Chinese characters are written with a space between each one and each character stands for a morpheme—the smallest meaningful unit in a language.

However, not every Chinese character stands for a word with full meaning, one that makes sense when used by itself. Many common words include bound morphemes, i.e., ones that cannot be used alone.

Characters are the most significant unit of the Chinese written language. Sentences consist of strings of monosyllabic characters (字), pronounced 'zi'. For this reason, Chinese is often thought to be a 'monosyllabic language'—a language composed of single-syllable words; this is of course not true.

There are many monosyllabic words in Chinese. Here are just a few examples:

人 pronounced 'ren', means *person*
吃 pronounced 'chi', means *to eat*
狗 pronounced 'gou', means *dog*
山 pronounced 'shan', means *mountain*
快 pronounced 'kuai', means *quick*
看 pronounced 'kan', means *to see*

Not every character can be regarded as a single word. There are countless Chinese words that consist of multiple syllables (polysyllabic), and the majority of them consist of two syllables (disyllabic).

Polysyllabic words may be inherently polysyllabic, i.e., they cannot be split into smaller units; or they may be the result of combining two or more monosyllables.

1) Some inherently polysyllabic words are:

珊 瑚 pronounced 'shanhu' and means *coral*
玫 瑰 pronounced 'meigui' and means *rose*

葡 萄 pronounced 'putao' and means *grape*
蜘 蛛 pronounced 'zhizhu' and means *spider*
玻 璃 pronounced 'boli' and means *glass*
糊 塗 pronounced 'hutu' and means *muddled*
尷 尬 pronounced 'ganga' and means *awkward*

The individual characters in these cases cannot be used in isolation and have no meaning. They are always used in tandem. There is no such thing as 玫, mei or 蜘, zhi and no one has ever been called 尷, gan or 尬, ga. Breaking these words up into individual characters would be like breaking the English word 'pigeon' into two words as 'pi' and 'geon'.

2) Combining two or more characters to form polysyllabic words is much more common than inherent characters.

This can be done by adding a suffix or prefix to a character, or in others, by combining meaningful characters to form 'compound' words.

Suffixes/Prefixes: Words that stood alone in Classical Chinese now add a suffix, especially in spoken language. The purpose of this is clear: to avoid confusion with the many homonyms. Suffixes include (子) zi, *child*, and (頭) tou, *head*.

Individual Characters		Word	Meaning
鼻 + 子 =	nose + child	鼻 子	*nose*
桌 + 子 =	table + child	桌 子	*table*
木 + 頭 =	wood + head	木 頭	*wood*

As you can see, the suffix is often obligatory. For example, 鼻 (bi) *nose* cannot be used on its own as a word, even though by itself it has the same meaning. The reason again is that by adding another character to form a word, chances of misunderstanding in speech are diminished, even though 子 or *child* does not add any meaning to it except to make it disyllabic.

Similarly, 木 (mu) by itself means *wood*, but it is not used on its own as a word in speech. It is always replaced by a more precise term such as 木材 (mu cai, *timber*).

Compound words are meaningful characters joined together to form larger words such as:

月亮 = moon + bright = *moon*
雲彩 = cloud + color = *cloud*

In everyday speech, many words that were monosyllabic have become disyllabic through this process. The purpose is obvious: to reduce misunderstanding.

There are thousands of other examples, including:

天氣 = sky + air = *weather*
明白 = bright + white = *to understand*
神秘 = divine + secret = *mysterious*
熊貓 = bear + cat = *panda*
動物 = to move + things = *animals*
路口 = road + mouth = *intersection*

Many characters never occur alone, always forming compounds with other characters. For example, 喜 (xi) *joy* and 歡 (huan) *pleasure* are put together to form the word 喜歡 (xihuan) *to like*. Both characters only occur in combination with other characters, in words such as 喜悅 (xiyue) *joy*, *pleasure* and 歡迎 (huanying) *welcome*. They would never occur by themselves as 喜 (xi) or 歡 (huan). Neither has full autonomy as a word.

Although Chinese is often mistaken as a monosyllabic language, primarily due to the appearance of the characters with spaces between them, we can see that it is indeed polysyllabic.

11

Did the Chinese Language Contribute to China's Decline?

Francis Bacon claimed that what he considered the three most important inventions—gunpowder, the magnetic compass and paper and printing—helped the West's transformation from the Dark Ages to the modern world. They were all invented by the Chinese.

The history of science and technology in China is both rich and varied and began over two thousand years ago. Between the first century BCE and the fifteenth century CE, Chinese civilization was much more efficient than the West in applying human natural knowledge to practical human needs. It was during this period that many technologies were developed. On the whole, it was a small, educated class who pursued science, passing down their understanding in books. Technology was a matter of craft and manufacturing skills that craftsmen derived from experience and privately transmitted to their children and apprentices.

The amazing part of the China's discoveries and inventions is that most were well documented, and in a writing that could be read even over a thousand years later.

Simon Winchester's bestseller, *The Man Who Loved China*, tells the tale of the famed Cambridge professor and scientist, Joseph Needham, who went to China (1942–1946) to document the sciences and inventions there. Eventually, Needham published a total of 27 volumes (*Science and Civilization of China*) describing China's contributions in all areas of science and technology.

In the volume on medicine, he described the Chinese system of using herbs. He also explained how the Chinese treated fractures and dislocations, the use of physiotherapy, acupuncture and moxibustion (cupping). Detailed drawings were uncovered, done over 2,000 years ago, of the circulation tracts and loci for acupuncture and moxibustion.

Acupuncture has been studied extensively by Western scientists and was determined to be effective in the control of pain, which can be explained with the gate theory of pain. Studies have also shown that it can stimulate the immune system to fight diseases, explained by the release of chemical signals in the body.

In addition, many nutritional deficiency diseases like goiter, beriberi, night blindness and rickets were described in great detail and the treatment given.

While in China, Needham was in a temple in Chongqing one day and found a heap of forgotten books, and discovered a fourth-century text containing materials unknown to Western historians of chemistry. Even though the text was written over a thousand years ago, Needham was able to read it. We can conclude from this that the Chinese written language has served China well for many years. When one considers the many dialects spoken throughout China, it's amazing that anyone who can read would be able to read that fourth-century text.

The herb qinghaosu (sweet wormwood) was described in a 400 CE text and recommended for the treatment of Malaria. Based on this information, in a writing that could be read by modern Chinese, the herb was refined and the drug Artemisinin was developed. It is now the most effective drug known to treat Malaria and won Chinese researcher Dr. To Youyou a Nobel Prize in 2015. She was able to read a notebook written by someone 1,600 years ago, and, remarkably, get useful information from it, proving once again the continuity of the language. Although centuries passed and dynasties came and went, the language survived.

During the Ming Dynasty, China, under Zheng He, launched seven missions to explore the world. The first voyage, from 1405 to 1407, involved 317 vessels and 26,800 men. The mission included men of all sorts of expertise: scientists, historians and engineers. The fleet sailed as far as Africa and Arabia. Such massive and complicated expeditions would have required detailed planning and a complex writing system to go with it.

Around 1500, China adopted an isolationist policy toward trade. At the same time, the population had grown exponentially. Then came the natural disasters, climatic changes, plagues and rebellions, all of which destabilized the country and made life miserable for many Chinese people. Such conditions were certainly not conducive to learning and making discoveries.

Things didn't improve during the Qing dynasty (1644–1911), a foreign rule by the Manchu. With more famines, floods and other natural disasters, rebellions and foreign invasions, most Chinese families merely tried to survive. They lived from crisis to crisis. Learning remained stagnant. In spite of being ruled by the Manchus for over 300 years, China retained the same writing system, with the Manchus adopting the language and giving up their own! Now the Manchu language is extinct with the exception of a few academics.

By the end of the 19th century, China was described as 'the sick man of Asia' because it had fallen so behind in science and technology, and the Chinese people were suffering from all sorts of ills. Many Chinese were addicted to opium. The country was occupied by various foreign powers and its people were subjugated and humiliated. The decline was so serious that many intellectuals thought the Chinese were not evolving as fast as the Westerners (Charles Darwin's theory of evolution was popular at this time). They believed that the Chinese were indeed inferior to Westerners.

With the population continuing to grow, progress in innovation saw diminishing returns. Europe had a smaller population but began to integrate science and technology that arose from the scientific revolution in the 17th century, giving Europe an advantage in developing technology in modern times. The West also had the benefits of discoveries made by the Arabs and Indians and, of course, the Chinese.

Another reason the West's science and technology advanced much more quickly than China's was its university system, which China did not have, and the related publication of new discoveries. Isaac Newton entered Cambridge University in 1661 and received a scholarship so that he could devote his life to new discoveries and teaching. The West had the resources to cultivate new scientists and provided them with the right environments to thrive.

Western mathematics and mathematical astronomy were introduced to China around 1600. Several Chinese scholars, realizing how behind they were, quickly began reshaping the way astronomy was studied in China. They came to believe for the first time that mathematical models could explain the phenomena as well as predict them. But there were so few scholars at the time that there was little they could do to change the system.

Some academics believed that one of the reasons for China's decline in science and technology was the imperial civil service examination system, which tested the candidates not on useful knowledge but on classics such as Confucian ideals. In Europe, the merchant class had supplied the world with many new ideas and inventions. (Charles Darwin never had to work for a living. He simply stayed home and pondered the world and life and did experiments! He was able to live off inheritances from his and his wife's families.) In traditional Chinese society, the merchants were presumed to be the lowest of the four social ranks. As a result, every merchant's son wanted to be a scholar and enter the imperial examination, hoping to move up in the bureaucracy, which provided power and prestige. All the best talents were drawn into civil service, and science and technology continued to decline.

Many thought China was behind because of its archaic writing system, which is incompatible with modern science and technology.

While the Western world marched on, China remained stagnant for a few centuries. Inventors tried for decades to come up with a Chinese typewriter. One was never invented that the average person could use, because of the large number of characters and complex components of their parts. Several were manufactured for industry and businesses, but the typist had to have taken special classes to operate the machine. It was so cumbersome that the Western press ridiculed it in a cartoon showing it as a technological monstrosity with six Chinese men working on one typewriter. Over the 20th century, the typewriter essentially remained unusable for the average person. Many saw it as proof that the Chinese characters were incompatible with the demands of the modern information age.

The digital age changed all that. I can now type Chinese characters on my computer, although it is still a slow process. I have to initially use the Pinyin system to get the sound of the character I wish to type. The computer then presents a list of characters with similar sounds, from which I pick the character I wish to type. It is still impractical compared to typing English or any other alphabet-based language, but at least I can now type in Chinese. The irony is that in the end, I still have to depend on the alphabet to type Chinese characters!

Until the 1970s, telegram was the most common way to send information over long distances in China. The problem with sending a telegram in Chinese was obvious with the Morse coding system. The solution was to convert the characters into four-digit numerical codes running from 0111 to 9999. The codebook consisted of about 7,000 commonly used Chinese characters. The characters were organized in standard dictionary order, each assigned a code.

The Morse Code assigns a set of dots and dashes or short and long pulses to each letter of the English alphabet. Transmission of such messages can be done over great distances. Even though the Morse Code is not used often now, it remains a viable means of providing highly reliable communication during difficult communication conditions.

To transmit a telegram, the operator had to look in the codebook for the four-digit number assigned to each Chinese character, and then transmit them in standard Morse signals. The receiving operator would then use the same codebook to decipher each of the characters. In contrast, a person sending a message in English would only have to worry about the 26 letters, numbers and a few symbols.

This is another example of how Chinese characters are not compatible with the modern age. Advances in technology have almost eliminated the use of the telegram, but all the new advances still rely on the alphabet system, in which the foundations of modern science are based. The entire field of information technology itself is alphabet based.

But Japan, with a writing system similar to the Chinese, had no problem adopting the science and technology of the West. So language alone could not account for China's decline.

Foreigners' views of the Chinese language have been varied over the years. Many Western scholars began studying the Chinese language in the twentieth century. Geniuses like Joseph Needham had no problem learning it. Many others worked hard at it and had reasonable success, and treated the task as an intellectual challenge. As they learned the correct strokes that composed each character, their fascination grew.

Some came to hate it and despised the language, which they found unlearnable. Some were convinced that the whole language was some kind of plot to snare the unwary and even to drive them mad.

Most scholars today feel that China's decline has been due to many factors, including the lack of property rights, the control of all aspects of life by the state, and China's failure to shift from an experience-based technological invention process to an experiment-based innovation process. It is beyond the scope of this book to discuss all of them, but China's difficult writing system certainly did not help. As I alluded to earlier, illiteracy was very high in China because of the time and resources involved in learning to read and write.

The truth of the matter is that civilizations rise and fall. We can see this in the case of the Islamic civilization, which at its peak was the world leader in mathematics. It gave the world the practical and functional numerical system, without which the world wouldn't be where it is today.

Some scholars feel that it is not that China fell behind, but it was the West that advanced science and technology at a speed never before seen in mankind's history. Ultimately, although China's character system is complex and not ideally suited to modern global advancements, the language is not as responsible for the country's decline as some might believe.

12

Can Studying Chinese Prevent Dementia?

Alzheimer's disease is caused by damage to connections between neurons in the brain. Because of the large number of sufferers and the severity of the debility, many top scientists are racing to try to find a cure, or some form of prevention. In spite of herculean efforts, so far nothing seems promising, although some drugs have shown to be effective in lessening the severity of the symptoms in the early and mid-stages. One potential solution would be to replace the damaged neurons with new ones to enable the patient to function for as long as possible.

Contrary to early neurological studies, the brain is more pliable than once believed, and it can generate new neurons if given proper stimulation. One of the exercises people are encouraged to do is to learn new things, such as a new language.

By using special brain scans and electrophysiology, scientists now can reveal what is happening in our brains when we hear, understand and produce second languages. In Sweden, scientists have found that learning a foreign language can increase the size of one's brain.

They have also discovered why adult native speakers of a language like Chinese cannot easily hear the difference between the English 'r' and 'l' sounds, thus making it difficult for them to distinguish words like 'river' and 'liver'. As discussed earlier, a single phoneme (sound unit) represents both sounds in Chinese. When subjects were presented with English words containing either of these sounds, the imaging studies of Chinese speakers showed only one area of the brain being activated, whereas in English speakers, two different areas of activation show up, one for each unique sound.

In order for Chinese speakers to hear and produce the differences between the two phonemes in English, they would have to undertake special exercises, listening to exaggerated 'r' and 'l' sounds to help rewire certain elements of the brain's circuitry.

Similarly, when studying Chinese, English speakers have to learn to differentiate new sounds like the tones. Challenging the brain to do this will grow neurons and establish new connections, increasing its capacity.

According to science writer Yudhijit Bhattacharjee, modern research suggests that while the interference of one language over another does exist, it appears that this continual switching is actually good for us. By improving the brain's executive function responsible for both focusing and alternating among key tasks, it forces the brain to resolve internal conflicts, strengthening the mind's cognitive capabilities.

Several articles have been published recently suggesting that learning a second language could even delay the onset of Alzheimer's disease and dementia. This theory has no scientific proof thus far, but the logic follows that anything helping the brain to work better is good for it.

It has also been suggested that studying a second language like Chinese would do even more for the brain than another language with an alphabet system similar to English. This is because a very different part of the brain would be used, i.e. rewired. New evidence suggests that the process of writing Chinese, counting each stroke, may train a whole array of cognitive abilities not utilized by the study of other languages and writing systems. Researchers at the Wellcome Trust in the UK found that Mandarin speakers use both temporal lobes when using this language, whereas English speakers only use their left temporal lobes.

In addition, learning to write Chinese characters aids the development of motor skills, learning shapes and letters, and the visual identification of graphics, all of which keep the mind sharp. Chinese characters are more complex than most other systems, because writing them involves strokes in all four directions: up, down, left and right. English, by contrast, is linear. In the sequential movement of the fingers and hand to form a character, the brain develops a functional specialization that integrates sensation, movement control and thinking. Imaging studies reveal that multiple areas of the brain become co-activated when a subject is learning to write Chinese characters.

Evidence also suggests that learning Chinese tones represents an added dimension to language learning, which probably requires extensive rewiring of certain elements in the brain, increasing its capacity, and perhaps helping it solve problems more efficiently than someone who knows just one language. All other written languages currently in use came from a single ancestor, which was developed in the Mesopotamian world several thousand years ago. Chinese characters represent a totally different form of writing; perhaps the new neural wiring would help the learner look at a problem in a different way.

By challenging the brain to learn a difficult language like Chinese, it is logical to assume that the increased capacity in brainpower could help to delay the onset of dementia.

13

Are Chinese Good in Math Because of the Language?

One stereotype of the Chinese is that they must be good in math. Is there any truth to it?

Several studies have shown that the majority of Chinese are indeed better at math than their Western counterparts. It is believed that this has a lot to do with the language.

According to Stanislas Dehaene, a renowned French neuroscientist and psychologist best known for his work in numerical cognition, Chinese number words are remarkably brief. Most can be said in less than one-quarter of a second. For example, 5 is 'wu' and 7 is 'qi'. Their English equivalents would be 'five' and 'seven', which are clearly longer; pronouncing them takes about one-third of a second each.

To demonstrate that Chinese can remember numbers better than Westerners, Dehaene suggests the reader look at a list of numbers such as: 7, 9, 6, 5, 3, 8, 4. Read them out loud to yourself then look away and spend 20 seconds memorizing that sequence before saying them out loud again.

An English speaker would have a 50 percent chance of remembering that sequence; but the Chinese would almost certainly be able to get it right nearly 100 percent of the time. This is because human beings store digits in a memory loop that runs for about two seconds. We can usually memorize whatever we can say or read within that two seconds. Chinese speakers get the list of number right every time because their language allows them to fit all seven numbers into two seconds. The English takes longer. The memory gap between Chinese and English is entirely due to the length of time it takes to think or say the numbers.

The people in Hong Kong who speak Cantonese, which has a quicker tempo of speech than Mandarin, can easily remember ten digits. This is more than any other language.

Dehaene explains that there is a big difference in how number-naming systems in English and Chinese are constructed. In English, we say *fourteen*, *sixteen*, *seventeen*, *eighteen*, and *nineteen* so naturally, you would think 11 should be one-teen, 12 should be two-teen and 13, three-teen. But instead they are *eleven*, *twelve*, *thirteen* and *fifteen*.

For 40 and 60, the English say *forty* and *sixty*. But for 20, 30 and 50, they say *twenty*, *thirty*, and *fifty*. There does not seem to be any logic in the system.

For English numbers above twenty, the 'decade' comes first and the unit number second: forty-one, fifty-two, etc. But for teens, it is the other way around with the decade second and the unit number first: fourteen, seventeen and so on.

The Chinese system seems more logical. Twelve is ten two and twenty-four is two ten four, and so on.

The difference between the two systems means that an average four-year-old Chinese child can count up to forty. An average four-year-old English-speaking child can only count up to fifteen. When a seven-year-old English-speaking child is asked to add twenty-seven plus thirty-one, that child has to convert the words to numbers (27+31). Only then can the child do the math: 1 plus 7 is eight and 30 plus 20 is 50, which makes 58. For the Chinese child, there is no need to break the numbers down; to add two-ten-seven and three-ten-one, the necessary equation is already there, embedded in the sentence.

Imaging studies have shown that native English and Chinese speakers use different parts of the brain when doing calculations. During the study, participants were asked to do simple addition problems such as 3 plus 4 equals 7. All subjects were working with Arabic numerals, which are used in both cultures.

Both groups were shown to engage a portion of the brain called the inferior parietal cortex, which is involved in quantity representation and reading. But the native English speakers also showed activity in the language processing areas of the brain, while native Chinese speakers used a brain region involved in the processing of visual information.

The researchers concluded that language definitely plays a role in math.

According to Karen Fuson, a Northwestern University psychologist, the Chinese number system is transparent. There is a pattern that can be followed without the need for rote learning. For fractions, the English would say two fifths, while the Chinese would say, 'out of five parts, take two', which is what a fraction is conceptually.

Chinese children can hold more numbers in their heads, and can do calculations faster. Fractions are not as confusing for them. These factors make them more likely to enjoy math. If they enjoy it, they may try harder and perhaps take more advanced classes, and they are more willing to do their homework—all of which contribute to their better performance.

Perhaps the Chinese language is especially suitable for math. There are critics who claim that because it takes longer for a Chinese speaker to be literate than someone whose language uses an alphabet system, it makes the Chinese student less creative.

There are advantages and disadvantages in all languages, and Chinese is one that is particularly suited to numbers and mathematics.

14

Idioms in the Chinese Language

Like English, the Chinese language has many proverbs and idioms, which are unique cultural components of the language. Proverbs are usually sayings that give advice such as 'Don't cry over spilled milk' and 'Those who live in glass houses shouldn't throw stones'. Chinese and English proverbs are very similar in that regard.

An idiom is a phrase that has a meaning of its own that cannot be understood from the meaning of its individual words, such as 'a canary in the coal mine' and 'by the skin of one's teeth'. Chinese idioms tend to be complicated and are often intimately linked with myth, story or historical fact. They almost always consist of four characters and their meaning usually surpasses the sum of the characters. Chinese idioms have been around for thousands of years, and therefore do not follow the usual grammatical structure and syntax of the modern Chinese spoken language, and are instead very synthetic and compact.

Foreigners learning Chinese often find the idioms frustrating because they are usually unintelligible without explanation. As with many languages, native Chinese speakers usually grow up hearing such idioms and have no problem understanding them.

In spite of some idioms having been created two or three thousand years ago, they are still common in vernacular Chinese writing and in the spoken language today. There are at least 5,000, many of which are redundant.

Here are some examples:

破釜沉舟 = po fu chen zhou = break woks, sink boats.

This is based on the historical account of the general Xiang Yu, who ordered his troops to destroy all of their own cooking utensils and boats after crossing a river into the enemy's territory. The battle was won because of this no-retreat strategy.

The following idiom is an example of a story that covered a span of over 2,000 years and involved well-known historical figures:

班門弄斧 = ban men nong fu = Ban's door, displays axe (i.e., showing off one's axe in front of Ban's door).

Lu Ban lived around the Spring and Autumn Period (770–476 BCE). He was a legendary carpenter, having invented various weapons and creating a number of carpenter's tools. He also helped build many famous palaces and was remembered as the best carpenter in Chinese history.

Li Bai (701–761 CE) was the famous Tang poet whose poem I quoted in chapter one. After his death, a beautiful tomb was built to honor him on the banks of the Caishi River. Admirers visited the tomb and many would write a poem or two on the tombstone.

One day during the Ming Dynasty (1368–1644), a scholar named Mei Zhihuan visited the tomb and was distressed to see the tombstone covered with poorly written poems. He decided to add one to the 'anthology', hoping it would discourage future visitors from adding more poems.

It read: 'A tomb near the Caishi River marks the everlasting fame of Li Bai; to and fro every passer-by writes a poem on the tombstone, just like an inferior carpenter trying to show off his proficiency with the axe before Lu Ban'.

Today, *Ban Men Nong Fu* is cited either to ridicule someone who displays pathetic skill before a master or to express one's modesty when demonstrating a skill in front of colleagues.

Without knowing these interconnected stories, one would have no idea what the idiom meant.

自 相 矛 盾 = zi xiang mao dun = self mutual spear shield.

This idiom comes from an ancient story about a vendor who bragged that the spear he was selling could pierce anything, and that his shield was impenetrable to any spear—an obvious contradiction. The meaning is to contradict oneself.

畫 蛇 添 足 = hua she tian zu = draw snake, add feet.

The meaning of this idiom is to ruin the effect by adding something superfluous. It too comes from an ancient story, but in this instance, even without knowing the story, one has a good idea of what it means.

塞 翁 失 馬 = sai weng shi ma = old man loses horse.

This is an idiom that every Chinese person knows. It comes from a story about a man whose horse ran away. He was very upset. But a year later, the horse returned with a herd. The man was happy. Then his son fell off the horse and broke a leg. The man was upset again. Soon, war broke out and all the young men in the area were drafted and most were killed. His son's life was saved because of the broken leg.

A setback may turn out to be a blessing in disguise.

對 牛 彈 琴 = dui niu tan qin = face cow play qin (a musical instrument). (i.e., To play qin to a cow.)

This very graphic idiom's meaning is obvious even without knowing the ancient story, as the cow would not appreciate the music. It means to address the wrong listener or waste your time by trying to explain something to a person who does not understand. This very common idiom is often used sarcastically, even by children.

瓜田李下 = gua tian li xia = melon field, beneath plums.

This idiom has a deeper meaning that implies suspicious situations. It is derived from a Han era poem, which includes the lines, 'Don't adjust your shoes in a melon field and don't tidy your hat beneath the plum trees'. The idiom consists of the first two characters of the two phrases: Gua tian bu na lu, li xia bu zheng guan.

It is highly visual and compact. It warns the reader to avoid situations in which, however innocent, he or she might be suspected of wrongdoing. The literal meaning of the idiom would be impossible to understand without the background knowledge of the phrase's origin.

名 落 孫 山 = míng luò sūn shān = name lower than sun shan.

This idiom is to used indicate that a person has failed an exam or lost a competition. The story is about Sun Shan, who took the Imperial Exam and managed to pass, but his name was last on the list. When he returned to his hometown, his neighbor asked him if his son had passed the same exam. Sun Shan replied that his own name was last on the pass list, and that the neighbor's son's name was below his, meaning that the son had not passed.

東施效顰 = dōng shī xiào pín = copying the beauty's frown.

Improper imitation that results in the opposite effect.

This is purported to be a true story. Xi Shi was a legendary beauty in ancient China. Sometimes she suffered from chest pains and walked around with a frown on her face. Many men thought the frown on this beauty's face actually made her more beautiful and desirable. In the same village, there was an ugly girl who heard the men commenting on how beautiful Xi Shi looked when she frowned and decided to imitate her. She walked around with a big frown on her face, which made her even uglier, and she became the laughingstock of the village.

刻舟求劍 = kè zhōu qíu jiàn = notch the boat to find the sword.

This is used to describe someone as being inflexible, unable to adapt to new situations. A man accidentally dropped his sword over the side of a boat. He immediately made a mark on the side of the boat where the sword was dropped and tried looking for the sword using the mark.

老馬識途 = lǎo mǎ shí tú = old horse knows the way.

This idiom is about the value of experience. An army had fought a tough battle and was returning from a long journey. A big snowstorm had covered the trail and other landmarks. The soldiers panicked, but the general assured them that all they had to do was follow the old horses, which eventually led them home.

騎虎難下 = qí hǔ nán xià = riding a tiger is difficult to dismount.

To be in a difficult situation but have to continue anyway, because stopping would be worse—just like trying to dismount from a ferocious tiger would be more difficult than staying on its back. There's a similar saying in English about having the tiger by the tail.

黔驴技穷 = qián lú jì qióng = donkey has used up all its tricks.

When one has exhausted all of their skills and nothing can be done to salvage the situation, much like a helpless donkey that has kicked and brayed to scare off a tiger and there is nothing more it can do.

三人成虎 = sān rén chéng hǔ = three men talking create a tiger.

Anything repeated enough times will soon be believed. A man was told by another that there was a tiger running loose on the street, attacking people. The man refused to believe it. A second man came along and told him the same thing; he was still unconvinced. Then a third man came to report that there was a tiger on the street, at which point the man finally believed the story.

守株待兔 = shǒu zhū dài tù = waiting by a tree stump for rabbits.

This idiom comes from a satirical story about a man who waits for luck and chance rather than working hard to get what he wants. A farmer was working in the fields when he saw a rabbit, running at full speed, hit a tree stump head on and break its neck. The farmer took the rabbit home to feed his family. He was convinced that all he had to do was wait beside the tree stump and rabbits would run into it for him to collect. He gave up farming and waited for the rabbits instead; but of course no more came.

同 舟共 濟 = Tòng zhōu gòng jì = crossing river in the same boat.

This is about putting aside differences in a time of crisis and working together. Two warring states shared a common river. One day, a storm arose and threatened the ferryboat loaded with people from both states. The people decided to put their differences aside and work together to keep the boat afloat. It's akin to the English saying, 'We're in the same boat'.

圖 窮 匕 见 = tú qióng bǐ xiàn = unrolling the map reveals the dagger.

Truth and intention are revealed when things arrive at the final stage. This is supposed to be a true story about the First Emperor Qin. An assassin in the guise of a diplomat went to see the Emperor to discuss the land that another state was ceding to him. He had hidden a dagger inside a rolled up map that was supposed to show the land being ceded. As the assassin unrolled the map, the Emperor saw the light reflection of the dagger and foiled the attempt. The assassin was killed.

臥 薪 尝 胆 = wò xīn cháng dǎn = sleep on firewood and taste gall.

To motivate oneself and work very hard to accomplish one's goals. A general lost a battle and was captured by the enemy. He labored as a slave for years, and after he was released, he vowed to seek revenge. To remind himself of his goal and the hardship he had suffered, he slept on firewood and tasted bitter gall before each meal. After ten years of training and hard work, he was able to defeat his enemy.

掩 耳 盜 鈴 = yǎn ěr dào ling = plug one's ears to steal a bell.

Ignoring realities to deceive oneself. A man attempted to steal a large bell from the temple but had to stop because of the noise while moving it. He decided to cover his ears, thinking that others, too, would not hear the noise.

魚 目 混 珠 = yú mù hùn zhū = pass off fish eyes as pearls.

During the Han dynasty, a sage wrote his formula for an elixir of immortality, which included grinding pearls into powder. He warned against substituting the pearls for something similar-looking like fish eyes.

指 鹿 為 馬 = zhǐ lù wéi mǎ = calling a deer a horse.

Denying the obvious; distorting facts. A chief minister in the Qin dynasty plotted to usurp. He was worried about the loyalty of the other ministers and devised a test. Before the court, in front of all the ministers, he pointed to a deer and asked the emperor what he thought of the horse. The emperor laughed and said it was not a horse but a deer. The prime minister then turned to all the ministers and asked them if it was a horse or deer. Some said it was a horse, some said it was a deer, and others kept silent. After the minister took over as emperor, he killed all those who had not agreed with him.

There are some idioms that are not derived from any stories. For example:

一 日 三 秋 = one day, three autumns.

This means to be greatly missing someone; one day feels like three years.

Idioms are a big part of the Chinese culture, and they are intertwined with the country's history and folklore. Even as children, we would throw an idiom into our daily conversation here and there. The beauty of Chinese idioms is that they are so easy to remember, because all of them contain only four characters. The uniqueness of the Chinese writing system has made the idioms very visually descriptive and yet simple enough that even children can understand them.

Throughout history, idioms have influenced the psyche of the Chinese people and guided how they view life and the world. They are primarily teaching guides for everyday life. The idiom about the man and his horse cautions us not to be too overjoyed over something good, nor to be too distraught over something bad, because our fortunes may change. It's one that has helped me at times in my own life when I've been faced with something difficult, reminding me that something good may yet come out of a bad situation.

The idiom 'Ban's door, displays axe' reminds us to be humble and not to show off, which I believe is one of the defining characteristic of the Chinese people.

The Chinese idiom is a rich and sophisticated cultural product that is made possible by China's unique system of writing.

15

Hong Kong Cantonese and the Chinese Language

Recently, an unpopular politician in Hong Kong remarked that Cantonese is not a language but only a dialect. This prompted many rebukes, including one from Alex Lo, an author and a columnist for the *South China Morning Post.* He argued that while it is true that Cantonese is not officially considered a language, almost all linguists agree that it is indeed one, and that Cantonese has more right to be called a language than standard Mandarin. The Mandarin language was created for the Mongols and Manchus when they ruled China and is more recent in origin.

Cantonese is synonymous with the Yue dialect of Guangdong Province. It is the dialect spoken around Canton (Guangzhou), an old city that was the center of commerce in South China for centuries. Hence, the Cantonese dialect was the *lingua franca* for much of southern China, Hong Kong and parts of Southeast Asia.

The Yue language has a long and venerable lineage dating back to the kingdom of Yue (first century BCE), and along with the Hakka language is considered one of the languages of the Tang Dynasty, rather than standard Mandarin, which came much later. Cantonese people call themselves Tang people, their homeland Tang Mountain, and so on.

The Cantonese now spoken in Hong Kong is described as Hong Kong speech and is different from the Cantonese spoken in nearby Guangdong province. Prior to the arrival of British settlers in 1842, the inhabitants of Hong Kong mainly spoke the Dongguan-Bao'an dialect of Yue, as well as Hakka, Chiuchau and Tanka of Yue Chinese. These dialects are significantly different from Cantonese. After Hong Kong became a British colony, large numbers of merchants and workers moved to Hong Kong from the city of Canton, and Cantonese became the dominant spoken language.

In 1949, during the Communist takeover of China, over a million refugees flooded into Hong Kong before the government closed the border to halt the influx. Many of these refugees were not Cantonese speakers. When movement and communication between Hong Kong and Guangdong became minimal, the evolution of Cantonese in Hong Kong and the rest of Guangdong went in different directions. Hong Kong Cantonese became the *lingua franca* amongst the immigrants from different parts of China. Because of the long exposure to English, large numbers of English words were introduced into Hong Kong Cantonese, and the vocabularies of Cantonese in Mainland China and Hong Kong are now quite different. In a *laissez-faire* society, Hong Kong Cantonese has evolved in a similar fashion, i.e., as a free-for-all.

Growing up in Hong Kong, I had always pronounced the word for *you* as 'nei' clearly. When I heard people sometimes using 'nei' and others using 'lei', I thought there was something wrong with my hearing, or the language had changed in the five years I had been away. Then I learned that most Cantonese speakers couldn't differentiate between 'l' and 'n', resulting in people using 'nei' and 'lei' interchangeably. This gives them problems with English names like Nicole, which they pronounce as 'lek kou', and Nancy, which they pronounce as 'len si'.

Then I began to notice that other words were blurred, such as 'Guangdong speech' being pronounced as 'Gungdong speech', the word for *love* and a few others. I later learned that these are the result of 'lazy sounds' that happen in languages when people become careless with their pronunciation.

When I read the street sign in Mongkok (旺角), which I knew should be pronounced Wongkok, I thought it was another 'lazy sound'. I asked many of my classmates who were born in Hong Kong about it, but they had no idea why the sign said Mongkok when they all referred to it as Wongkok in speech. I later discovered that, indeed, Mongkok should have been Wongkok, but a Chinese sign maker over a hundred years ago got the first letter upside down, and the wrong name stayed.

As mentioned, Hong Kong speech is full of English words. In everyday conversation, even people who don't speak any English will mix English words with Chinese, such as asking 'nie hap mh hap pi?', meaning, *Are you happy?,* or 'nei su mh su aa?', meaning, *Are you sure?* Another common example is, 'ngo wui call nei', meaning, *I will call you.*

Similar to the way the English language has adopted some Chinese words, such as ketchup, kowtow, feng shui, kumquat, loquat, wonton, dim sum and bok choy, Hong Kong Cantonese contains many everyday words borrowed from English. A visitor to Hong Kong might hear words like 'baa si' for *bus*, 'dik si' for *taxi*, 'saam man zi' for *sandwich*, 'si do' for *store*, 'si do be lei' for *strawberry*, 'saam man yu' for *salmon*, 'bou fei' for *buffet* and 'saa leot' for *salad*, to name just a few.

Hong Kong people are not shy, and many of them think they can speak Mandarin simply by speaking Cantonese with a slightly different tone. This often creates confusing or hilarious situations. There is a story about a Hong Kong businessman at a Beijing hotel who lost one of his shoes and reported to the manager that his 'hai zi' was missing. In Mandarin, 'hai zi' (孩子) means *young child*, and *shoe* is 'xei zi' (鞋 子); but in Cantonese, *shoe* is 'hai'. After some initial excitement, it became clear that it was not his child that was missing but rather his shoe. I've witnessed many similar situations where a Cantonese speaker and a Mandarin speaker tried to communicate unsuccessfully, and found them especially funny because I know both dialects.

My mother was raised in Beijing and could speak impeccable Beijing-accented Mandarin, and I remember her repeating an old saying whenever she heard a Cantonese speaker struggling with Mandarin:

Tian bu pa	I don't fear Heaven
Di bu pa	I don't fear Earth
Jiu pu Guangdongren	I just fear Cantonese
Shuo Guanhua	Speaking Mandarin

Cantonese is so different from Mandarin that it certainly fits the criteria of being a separate language. It is a spoken language and many of its words are not found in the standard Chinese dictionary. Hong Kong people have invented many words to suit their speech, words that are known only to them. For example, the word for *elevator* (or *lift* in British English) is 'lib' (車立), which combines the radical for *vehicle* (車) and a phonetic component (立) with the syllable 'li'. This word is not found in the standard dictionary and no Mainland Chinese would have the faintest idea what it means. I came across it a few years ago while reading a Chinese newspaper in Hong Kong.

Cantonese vulgarity is especially colorful, and written words have been invented to go along with them. Swear words are commonly used by the lower class, and some people seem to have forgotten what they really mean and that they can be offensive. Some use swear words as a way to greet a friend, as if to say 'good morning', or to begin a sentence by insulting the other person's mother or family, and nobody seems bothered by it. Quite a few characters have been invented for these Cantonese swear words, such as combining the word for *door* (門) with a phonetic component 'xiao' (小), meaning *little*, which appears inside the character for *door* and is pronounced 'diu', creating the equivalent of a common English four-letter word.

When my mother's family returned to Canton after she finished high school, her mother had to remind her constantly not to use the word 丟 *or 'diu', which in Mandarin means 'to lose [something]'; in Cantonese, it is the most common swear word.*

There are other less offensive curse words like 'puk gai', which means *lying prostrate on the street*. It is an extremely common phrase that can be translated as *drop dead*, although I think it can sometimes be more sinister and malicious than that.

Another frequently heard curse word that is not vulgar is 'ham gaa chaan', which means *may your whole family be dead*. 'Chaan' means *shovel* or *to shovel*; it probably relates to a funeral and ultimately to the meaning of death. In Chinese culture it is not uncommon to curse a person as well as their family, something rarely done in Western culture.

In Hong Kong, there are laws that prohibit the usage of profanity in public, but I have never seen them enforced.

Hong Kong people are also known for their humor. Many colorful Cantonese expressions are only understood in Hong Kong. Below are some examples.

Gwo gaai louh syu = a rat crossing the street. Someone who is so hated that everyone wants to beat him up on sight.

Fan san hum yu = The salted fish comes alive. Someone who is washed-up and beyond hope but is able to make an incredible come back; usually refers to a financial comeback.

Gie tun ap kong = Chicken talking to a duck. Two people talking to each other with no idea what the other is saying.

Gwai dei wai jyu na = kneeling down to feed the sow. To put up with humiliations and insults in order to accomplish a goal.

Mou nga lou fu = toothless tiger. Someone who has no power.

Lou maau siu sou = old cat gets its whiskers burnt. When an expert makes a mistake.

Keh gnau wan mah = riding a cow to look for a horse. Working at one job while looking for a better one.

Gwan seui luk geuk = pour hot water on the feet. When a visitor is in a hurry to leave.

Gwat tau da gu = bone hitting the drum. Refers to someone who is long dead.

Cheuih fu fong pei = taking off trousers to pass gas. Doing something unnecessary.

Ga yim ga chou = add salt and vinegar. To embellish.

Joh sihk saan bang = sitting idle, one can eat up a mountain. One must work; otherwise, even a fortune would be gone.

Nga jai sihk wohng lihn = a deaf-mute eats yellow lotus [very bitter]. When someone has suffered a grievance but is unable to complain.

Sihk yuhn faahn = eat soft rice. When someone lives off of his wife or girlfriend; a gigolo.

Jum guo ham su '= has soaked in salt water. Refers to someone who has crossed the ocean for higher education.

Dai lok mo = wear a green hat. When someone is being cuckolded. There are several versions of the story behind this expression. The most accepted one is that an official's wife was having an affair, and to let her lover know when her husband was out of town, she would wear a green hat.

Sam cheung leung dyun = three long ones and two short ones. Misfortune that results in death. This refers to the Chinese coffin, which is made of three long pieces and two short pieces of wood with the top left open.

There are also some more common expressions that non-Cantonese speakers may understand, such as:

Chaau yau yu = fry squid. To get fired from a job. How this expression came about is impossible to trace.

Yen tau ju nou = human head, pig brain. A very stupid person.

Ngan hong = eyes red. Similar to the Western expression 'green with envy'.

Teet fan woon = iron rice bowl. When someone has a very secure job.

Gum fan woon = gold rice bowl. When someone has a very secure job with excellent pay.

Dah lan fan woon = break the rice bowl. Losing one's livelihood.

Jaang fan woon = fighting for rice bowl. Competing for jobs.

Yauh gon seui = swim without water. To play mahjong.

Dai wok = big wok. Big trouble.

Since 1997, when British rule in Hong Kong ended, many Mainland Chinese have settled in Hong Kong, and each year millions of Mainland Chinese tourists flock to the territory. The residents of Hong Kong, already stressed out by the high density population, resent the rich Mainlanders who bid up the real estate prices and the hordes of tourists who invade their living space. These factors, combined with their inability to communicate with each other, can make for some ugly confrontations. Hong Kong natives know who the Mainlanders are as soon as they open their mouths. With six tones, Cantonese is an extremely difficult language to learn. Adding to this the mixtures of English words, and expressions only known in Hong Kong, and it may as well be another country for the Mainland Chinese.

The residents of Hong Kong are proud of their culture and heritage, and many don't consider themselves citizens of China, preferring to call themselves Hong Kong people. Once an outsider, always an outsider in Hong Kong, especially because of the nuances of the language and culture. Even for someone like me, who lived in Hong Kong for many years, it was a struggle to blend in when I returned after living in Malaysia for five years. I consistently made the mistake of confusing the two versions of 'thank you' in Cantonese until someone pointed it out to me. To thank someone for a service is 'mh goi', such as thanking a waiter for bringing the food. But to thank someone for a gift is 'do jeh'. As you can see, someone cannot easily pretend to be a local in Hong Kong. The subtleties and unique features of the dialect make it a language all its own.

16

Names and the Chinese Language

Almost all Chinese names have a literal meaning. Chinese parents, like parents all over the world, have great expectations for their children, and they believe that by selecting a name with a good meaning, the child will live true to his or her name and thus have a good life. They may also choose names based on other positive elements, such as pleasing sounds or the beauty of the written character.

Children are frequently given names based on gender stereotypes. Boys' names will imply strength or courage while girls receive 'feminine' names concerning beauty or flowers. Historically, female names sometimes reflected ancient China's sexist attitudes, such as Laidi, Shaodi, or Pandi, which all essentially mean *Seeking a Little Brother*; or Yehao, meaning *Also Good.*

Names connected to current events or with political associations are also common. For example, according to a 1990 article in the *Times*, tens of thousands of men were named Li Jianguo (Build-the-Country Li), Wang Jun (Army Wang) and Zhang Hong (Red Zhang) after the Communists took over China. Other revolutionary names include Qiangguo (Strong Nation) and Dongfeng (Eastern Wind). Such a name offers an instant clue as to when the person was born. A name like 'Build the Country' probably belongs to a person born between 1949 and 1950; and Yuanchao, meaning *Assist Korea*, is a common name for those born during the Korean War. Chaoying, 'Surpass England', is likely someone born in the late 1950s when Mao Ze

Dong began an effort to catch up with Western industry. A person named Weidong, meaning *Protect Mao Ze Dong*, was probably born during the Cultural Revolution.

China Daily, the official Chinese newspaper, approvingly reported that one soldier named his child Pingbao, meaning *Suppress Rioting*, in honor of the crackdown against the Tiananmen Democracy Movement in 1989!

Although current laws in China state that babies must be registered within a month of being born, children were traditionally named a hundred days after birth. Until the child's formal name is decided upon, many parents use a 'milk name' that uses double characters or a diminutive such as xiăo ('little'). Some families superstitiously use disgusting or unappealing milk names, such as Bóng-chhī ('No Takers') or Ti-sái ('Pig Feces'), to let evil spirits and bad omens know that the babies are not worth their attention.

Before the 20th century, educated Chinese used what was known as zì (字), or a 'courtesy name', which was a name they were known by outside of their close friends and family members once they reached maturity. The practice was based on a statement in the ancient Chinese *Book of Rites* that claimed it was disrespectful among adult peers to use given names for each other. These names, also known as 'style names', were typically assigned to men at the age of twenty, although some women assumed them upon marriage, and they were commonly given to women during the Zhou dynasty as well, when the practice was first becoming widespread. Courtesy names were often decided upon by parents or teachers, although they were sometimes self-assigned. They were often connected to the formal name either by a similar meaning or quality. They could also be a simple homophone, or might display birth order in the bearer's family.

Although the practice of courtesy names was largely abandoned after the anti-imperialist May the Fourth movement of 1919, the Chinese people still maintain many traditions around naming. It is still considered inappropriate within many families to use the given names of elder relatives. Instead, you will often hear family members refer to each other using names that identify their place in the family hierarchy, such as Big Sister, Second Brother, etc. References to relationships with extended family include whether the connection is by birth or marriage and if it's on the mother's or father's side.

Because using a given name traditionally indicates the speaker's authority or position of power, emperors would often have six or more names they were called in different situations by different people. Much like we wouldn't refer to the Queen of England as 'Liz' or 'Elizabeth', but more likely 'Your Highness' or 'Your Majesty', Chinese subjects would use the appropriate name for an emperor as indicated by their station. People with the same name as an emperor—or sometimes even just a homophone—would often be made to change their names.

In addition to the names used during their lifetimes, royalty and some prominent members of court received honorary posthumous names (shìhào).

While many languages use gender to determine titles, such as Mr., Mrs., Ms., etc. in English, the Chinese frequently use a person's occupation as a titular sign of respect. A recognizable example might be Mao Ze Dong's title as Chairman Mao, rather than Mr. Mao or something similar. Teachers are held in high regard in China, so a teacher with the surname Li would be called Lǐ Lǎoshī (Teacher Li). Similarly, engineers are often addressed by their job titles, and heads of companies may be referred to as zǒng, meaning *general* or *overall.* Another common title is 'Manager'.

On a much less formal scale, nicknames occur in China much as they do in Western cultures. Some use self-assigned pseudonyms, called hào ('art names'), or pen names (bǐmíng). An example is the exiled poet Zhao Zhenaki, whose bǐmíng is Bei Dao, meaning *North Island.*

Some other nicknames are acquired in childhood or youth, assigned by family or friends. Frequently, Chinese nicknames are derived from someone's physical appearance or behavior, or perhaps a quirk of their speaking style. Names like 'Little Fatty' aren't as offensive as we find them in their English translations; and even names using the word lǎo (*old*) aren't considered insulting, particularly since elders are highly respected in Chinese culture. Other common nicknames frequently reference animals.

Because secondary schools in China teach English to prepare students for the required English language component of the college entrance exam, many teenagers adopt English names, which many of them keep and use as nicknames. They can be appealing because they are easier to use with foreigners who struggle with the tones of the Chinese language, and many people in China see foreign names as more modern and egalitarian. These names are sometimes chosen for their sounds or associations that don't necessarily translate as nicknames English speakers would use. Surprisingly common names include Chlorophyll, Candy, Devil and Whale.

Chinese names consist of a surname (xìng—almost always contains one character, rarely two) and a given name (míng). Unlike Western names, the Chinese surname comes first. Given names traditionally consist of two syllables, though it is not uncommon to use only one. They may be chosen based on the meanings of each individual character, but the name is always a single unit. However, when two-syllable given names are transcribed into English, they can be written as one name or separately, such that Mao Zedong and Mao Ze Dong are both correct.

Many Chinese historical figures had given names with a single character, such as the immortal Tang Dynasty poet Li Bai. Almost all the characters in the Chinese classic *Romance of the Three Kingdoms* had given names containing one character, such as Liu Bei, Guan Yu and Zhang Fei. However, more than 80% of Chinese names consist of two characters.

While many Western parents honor their families by naming children after their relatives, the Chinese have a taboo against it that dates back at least as far as the Shang dynasty, and they avoid using the names of ancestors and elders out of fear and respect. Instead, many Chinese names reflect familial connections through a system of 'generation name', which is a common name given to all children of a generation, such as siblings, cousins, etc. In a two-character given name, usually the first and sometimes the second character is shared. For example, Mao Ze Dong had two brothers. Their names were Mao Ze Min and Mao Ze Tan, with all three sharing the common characters Mao and Ze.

In my own family, my given name is Yum Yuen and my brothers' names are Ting Yuen and Chung Yuen, with all of us sharing the second character Yuen (遠).

There is a tremendous difference between one-character and two-character given names in regard to the problem of duplication. With a two-character given name, and with 50,000

Chinese characters, the combination possibilities are almost limitless. From my personal experience, given names with two characters have never caused any confusion, as I have never come across anyone with a name identical to mine.

During the last few decades, there has been a trend in naming children with one character. (This coincides with the onset of the one child policy. Perhaps there is no longer the need to take a 'generation name' into account as they all have just one child.) This has created a problem because of the paucity of Chinese surnames. In spite of the existence of more than 4,000 Chinese surnames, a slang term for the Chinese people is Bǎijiāxìng (百家姓)—*Hundred Family Surnames*—because only a hundred surnames comprise over 85% of the population. The top ten surnames—Zhang (Chang), Wang (Wong), Li (Lee), Zhao, Chen (Chan), Yang (Young), Wu (Ng), Liu (Lau), Huang, and Zhou—are used by 40% of Chinese, more than 500 million people.

Some characters are spelled differently depending on the dialect; for example, Wang in Mandarin and Wong in Cantonese share the same character of 王.

When Chinese parents decide to use only one character for the given name of their child, they often select a character with an auspicious meaning such as *Great*, *Brave*, and *Strong* for boys and *Virtue*, *Tranquil* and *Beautiful* for girls. As a result, there are almost 300,000 Chinese men with the identical name Zhang Wei (張偉), which means *Zhang the Great.*

This has created a nightmare for the Chinese Public Security Bureau. With so many Chinese having identical names, the Bureau often arrests the wrong person. It can cause problems in daily life as well, such as when a common name like Zhang Wei (張偉) is announced over the PA at an airport or train station, there can be three or four people rushing to answer to the name.

This problem is compounded by the homonyms in the language, as syllables like 'zhang' and 'wei' are also shared by a long list of characters. Zhang or 張 is shared with 長, 章, 仗, 丈, 帳 or 嶂, among many others; and 'wei' is shared with 偉, 為, 位, 未, 威, 維, 微, 尾, 衛 or 圍, and more.

When the PA announces Zhang Wei's name, it could be 張偉, the most common name in China, or other less common combinations such as 長為, 章位, 仗未, and a long list of other names that sound identical even though the characters are totally different.

The combination of the most common surnames with the most common one-character given names means that, in addition to the 300,000 Zhang Wei's in China, there are also 290,000 Wang Wei's, 270,000 Li Wei's, and 240,000 Liu Wei's.

For some reason, the Chinese love the two-character 秀英 ('Xiuying'), meaning *Outstanding Beauty* for their daughters. As a result, there are a quarter million Wang Xiuying's, Li Xiuying's and Zhang Ziuying's. A common one-character female given name is Li (麗), meaning *beautiful*. There are over 200,000 Zhang Li's and Wang Li's, and 170,000 Li Li's in China!

The small number of Chinese surnames has led to confusion in social environments. Some Chinese parents who desire individuality give their children unusual names, but sometimes these names are so unusual that most people cannot read them and the person constantly has to explain the sound and meaning of their name character(s). Of the approximate 50,000 Chinese characters used in China, only about 32,000 of them are programmed into the computers used by the Chinese government. The government has asked these individuals with unusual names to change them so they can get new computer-readable public identity cards.

Using obscure characters to avoid duplication of names is not a solution, since most people don't know these characters and are perplexed by them, and computers cannot read them, resulting in great inconvenience to everyone, including the bearer of such a name.

Undoubtedly, policy-makers in China must be making a tremendous effort to solve this problem. Perhaps they should take the mother's surname into consideration, as the Portuguese do. For example, if one Zhang Wei's maternal surname is Li, his name would be Zhang Li Wei. If another Zhang Wei's maternal surname is Wang, then his name would be Zhang Wang Wei. With this system, the Chinese Public Security Bureau would have a much better chance of arresting the right person!

17

Character Amnesia and the Chinese Language

As I bid goodbye to my high school friend Michael at the Hong Kong Jockey Club after breakfast, I asked him if he could write down the Chinese name of a restaurant for me—the Golden Bauhinia. Our alumni association was having a luncheon the following Saturday, and I wanted something to show the taxi driver should I get lost. He took out his pen and began writing, but stopped at the last character and apologized that he had forgotten how to write it. As I mentioned earlier, I didn't have trouble learning all the characters, but I do have a hard time remembering how write some of them.

What Michael and I have in common is something that is happening to millions of other Chinese: character amnesia, a phenomenon whereby experienced speakers of the Chinese language forget how to write Chinese characters that were previously well known to them. In Chinese it is known as 'pick up pen, forget the character' or 提筆忘子. This phenomenon is tied to prolonged use of electronic gadgets; but in my own case, it is simply an issue of not writing more often. Users of electronic gadgets usually use Romanization to input Chinese characters using their phonetic transcriptions, without having to know how to write them by hand.

The background of Chinese characters has been covered in previous chapters. The characters can be very complex, and learning them is a highly neuromuscular task. Remembering them is not easy without repetitive practice in writing them by hand. Being able to recognize and being able to write a character are two very different things. It is much easier for the brain to recognize previously learnt characters; but in order to write them from memory, the brain needs a greater capacity.

It's difficult to estimate how many different Chinese characters are in use today. A widely used proficiency test for Chinese as a second language tests over 2,600 different characters. A recent published list of commonly used characters in China contains 7,000 different characters. As a result of people using computers and other devices more and more, fewer people are writing Chinese by hand. Many are no longer exposed to the reinforcement needed to retain the ability to write these characters.

With the advent of the World Wide Web in 1991, and widespread use of email, discussion forums and Internet chat, people began to use computers and smart phones to communicate with each other in Chinese script. The common use of SMS (Short Message Service) text messaging means that a large portion of these people's everyday use of Chinese characters utilizes input methods not done by hand. Input methods based on phonetic transcription are now the most popular forms of communication, and users do not have to know how to write the characters.

The more devices people own (smart phones, tablets, computers, etc.), the less often they go through the elaborate sequences of strokes that make up Chinese characters. Most Chinese use a system whereby they type out the sound of a word in Pinyin—the most commonly used Romanization system—and they are instantly given a list of characters to choose from.

One of the reasons for the tremendous economic progress in China during the last two decades is its adoption of IT. China is second, after the US, in industrial output, and has become an IT giant in which social media and smart phones are common tools for its people. Some Chinese feel that perhaps their language is not incompatible with the IT world after all, as has been suggested in the past, because the Chinese language has become one of the most commonly used languages on the Internet. A massive and concerted effort on the part of computer programmers has been made for almost three decades to put Chinese character input on par with that of alphabetic systems. The most common input methods are still cumbersome in comparison with typing in alphabetic text. *Pinyin or handwriting input on a smart phone or IPad still generally involves a two-step process in which the user must pick the correct character candidate from a pop-up menu.*

Some scholars go as far as to say that Chinese script has conquered the alphabet system. This is of course not true. The alphabet system is still what drives IT. Chinese script can be used on the Internet because of decades of very hard work and ingenuity to figure out a way to input thousands of complex characters using the limited key set of the regular keyboard. The success of Chinese script on the Internet is not due to the Chinese writing itself, but more because of the ingenuity and cleverness of the countless programmers who devised the solutions.

The fact remains that years of hard work are still required to memorize a few thousand characters to be literate in the Chinese language. If a Chinese person does not have a command of those two or three thousand characters, he or she wouldn't be able to communicate on the Internet; whereas an

English speaker only needs to know the 26 letters of the alphabet.

Recently, speech-to-text technology has been improved so much that it is possible to simply talk into a smart phone, and it will produce the text in Chinese characters. Programs now exist that will convert Cantonese and Mandarin speech into text. More and more Chinese are using this technology, which means that fewer people are inputting the characters on their devices. This will most likely further exacerbate the problem of character amnesia.

In 2013, a Chinese TV program hosted a spelling bee contest. In one instance, only 30% of participants were able to write the word 'toad' (Lai hai ma in Pinyin; Chinese: **癞 蛤 蟆**). You might think 'toad' is a common word that most Chinese should be able to write, but the spelling bee proved otherwise. The problem has gotten so bad among young people that the government media have produced several TV shows in which middle school children compete in various character writing challenges as a way of reviving the rapidly deteriorating of skills of writing by hand.

Ironically, this character amnesia phenomenon is the result of relying on the less memory intensive alphabetic Pinyin system. In the end, users still have to resort to the alphabet-based Pinyin system to check their digital dictionaries to retrieve the forgotten character, or simply opt out of the system entirely, bypassing having to write anything by using some kind of speech-to-text technology to get the right character on the screen.

Computer technology has made great strides in solving the problem of character entry, putting alphabets and Chinese characters on almost equal footing. Yet, there are still inefficiencies and added burdens that have always troubled the character writing system. In spite of the inefficiencies, it would be a shame to see a writing system with such aesthetic beauty and so steeped in China's history and culture fade away.

The truth is that there is no shortcut. Learning how to write Chinese will always be difficult, and trying to remember the several thousand characters requires writing them out on a regular basis. Otherwise, they will certainly be forgotten.

18

Superstition and the Chinese Language

An American friend of mine who was studying Chinese was puzzled to see a poster with the character for *good fortune*, 'fu' (福), hanging upside down in a Chinese restaurant during Chinese New Year. I explained to him that this is a result of Chinese superstition involving a play on the sounds of two homonyms in Chinese characters.

The Chinese characters 到 and 倒 both contain the syllable 'dao'. 到 means *to arrive* and 倒 means *upside down*. The idea is that this upside down (dao) picture of 'fu' will cause good fortune to arrive (dao) in the coming year.

Chinese society is rife with superstitious beliefs. Over the past few thousand years, such beliefs have allowed the Chinese people to feel that they have some control over their fates as dynasties have come and gone, and as all sorts of natural and man-made disasters like war, famine, and flood—things over which they have no control—have swept through their lives.

The superstitious aspects predominantly grew out of the Cantonese culture but have taken root in other dialects and regions as well. Many Chinese superstitions are based on homophones in the language, because numerous unrelated concepts are expressed with the same syllable sound.

Superstitious beliefs emerge when those unrelated concepts are linked.

For example, the bat is considered an emblem of good fortune to the Chinese because the word for *bat* is 'bian fu' (蝙蝠), containing the same sound as the word for *good fortune*, 'fu'. This homophonic connection has made the bat a common theme in Chinese folk art. Many homes display cut paper pictures or other depictions of bats, with the hope of attracting good fortune.

During Chinese New Year, many Chinese people include fish in their meals, as *fish*, 'yu' (魚), contains the same sound as 俞, which means *surplus*. Paintings and pictures of fish, especially koi fish of red or gold color—both are lucky colors—are often displayed in Chinese homes.

The Chinese New Year cake 'nian gao' is found in every home during Chinese New Year because the word for *New Year cake* (年 糕) consists of homonyms of 年 高, which means *higher each year* and can refer to one's job or the amount of one's wealth. In addition, lettuce is often served during New Year because 'sheng cai' (生 菜), *lettuce*, uses the same syllables as 生 財, which means *to give rise to wealth*.

A food that most Westerners are unfamiliar with is 'fa cai' (髮 菜), which the Chinese call 'hair vegetable' because it looks like black hair. It is really black algae that grows in the sandy soil of parts of Northwest China. It is always served during Chinese New Year because its sounds 'fa cai' are identical to 發 財, which means *to get rich*.

There are certain gifts that should never been given in China because of superstitious connections. In both Mandarin and

Cantonese, *giving a clock* contains the syllables 'song zhong' (送 鐘), which sound exactly like *paying one's last respects* (送 終). Giving someone a clock in China is the biggest taboo, as it might even be mistaken for a wicked curse, or, worse, as a declaration of war. In both Mandarin and Cantonese, a *bell* (鐘) is also called 'zhong', which is identical to *clock*, so it wouldn't be a good idea to give someone a bell either.

Should such a gift be given, the 'unluckiness' of the gift can be countered by exacting a small monetary payment so that the receiver is essentially buying the clock, which nullifies the 'giving' (送) part of the phrase. Instead, it would become *buying clock* or 'mai zhong', which is not unlucky. As an interesting cultural side note, watches make acceptable gifts.

An umbrella is another gift that should be avoided in China because *umbrella* (傘) with the syllable 'san' sounds like 散, which means *to break up*. *Fan* (扇), pronounced 'shan', also has a similar sound as *to break up* so it should also not be considered as a gift.

Book (書) is 'shu' in Mandarin and contains the same syllable as 輸, which means *to lose*. Similarly, in Cantonese, *book* and *to lose* share the same syllable. Hong Kong people like to gamble, so it is especially taboo as a gift. Unless you know your friend very well, a book would not be a good gift idea.

Giving shoes as a gift is considered bad luck as *shoe* (鞋) or 'xie' in Mandarin is the homophone of 邪, which means *evil*. The Chinese also believe that giving shoes equips a person to 'walk away' from a relationship. This only works in Mandarin as in Cantonese *shoe* is 'hai', which is not a homophone of *evil*.

Sharing a pear with loved ones or friends can be a mistake in China, as *sharing a pear* (分 梨) is a homophone of 分 離, which means *to separate.*

In addition, certain numbers are considered by some to be auspicious or inauspicious based on the Chinese word that the number sounds similar to. The number two is considered lucky because of the saying *good things come in pairs.* In Cantonese, *two* is 'yi', which sounds like *easy* (易)—as in easy money, easy life.

The Chinese believe that doubles bring blessings. Many decorations for celebrations are in pairs, and gifts are given in even numbers. Chinese wedding decorations often include the word 'xi' (喜), which means *happiness*, and repeating it as 'shuang xi' (喜喜) means *double happiness.*

The number 3, 'san' (三), sounds similar to the character for *birth* (生) and is considered a lucky number.

The number 6, 'liu' (六), sounds similar to the character for 'liu' (流), which means *to flow* or *road* and is also seen as a lucky number.

The number 7 is another lucky number. It is 'chut' in Cantonese, which symbolizes togetherness; and in Mandarin, it sounds like 'qi' (起), which means *arise.*

The number 8 is 'ba', which sounds similar to the word for *prosper* or *wealth* (發), and it is considered the luckiest number. The word also is phonetically similar to the word for *a hundred* (百), alluding to wealth and longevity. It's no surprise, then, that the Beijing Olympics commenced at 8:08 pm on August 8th, 2008 (8/8/08)!

Many businesses in the west take into account these cultural idiosyncrasies. Several real estate companies in Asia, Hawaii, Vancouver and the San Francisco area will list a house price that contains the number 8, such as $888,000 or $788,000, in order to attract Chinese buyers. Most airlines that have fights into China assign a flight number containing the number 8, such as flight UA8, BA88, AC88, KL888, UA888 and CX888. *(All of these are actual flight numbers.)*

The number 9, 'jiu' (九), is a homophone for 久, which means *long lasting*. It is yet another lucky number.

The number 4, 'si' (四), is viewed as a very unlucky number because it has the same sound as 死, which means *death*. In Beijing and Shanghai, one will never find People's Hospital Number 4, but one can find Hospitals Number 1, 2, 3 and 5. Associating a hospital with a symbol connected to death is definitely unwise. Even though the Communist Party has tried to get rid of superstition in China, these cultural beliefs run deep. Why go to Hospital Number 4 if you can go to Hospital Number 3 or 5 instead?

In Hong Kong, some high-rise residential buildings omit all floor numbers containing a 4 (e.g., 4, 14, 24, 34) and all floors from 40–49. In addition, they will often not have a 13th floor either, so a building with the highest floor numbered 50 may actually have only 35 physical floors!

This belief also extends to combination numbers such as 168, which goes with the syllables 'yi', 'liu' and 'ba' and sounds like 一 路 發, standing for 'one road prosper' and meaning *fortune all the way*. There are many other such examples.

This type of superstition is probably unique to the Chinese culture because of the countless homophones in the language.

19

Lost in Translation

When I was in high school in Hong Kong, we were required to take classes in translation for two years. This involved translating English texts into Chinese, and vice versa. It was not an easy task. In order to do a good job, the translator must be proficient in both languages. We were taught to fully understand the original text first, and then to try translating it into the other language the best we could, taking cultural contexts into consideration. We were warned against literal translation.

Language and culture are closely intertwined, as we've seen throughout this book. Many Chinese-to-English 'mistranslations' are not only amusing (and confusing!), but they also reveal more about the culture of the Chinese people. Additionally, the prevalence of poorly translated signage throughout China gives insight into the thinking of top-level and local governments, private entrepreneurs, and tourist bureaus, etc., which are responsible for producing these signs.

English is a language that, for the most part, relies heavily on logical sequences, whereas Chinese is deeply rooted in its graphic imagery, with very loose grammatical structures. When a translation is done literally, the result can be disastrous.

Chinglish occurs when the translator applies Chinese grammatical structures to an English translation. This is one of the ways a translation can become ridiculous.

Here are a few examples of Chinglish:

> **我 跟 我的 朋 友 一 起 吃 晚 飯** = wo gen wo de peng you yi qi chi wan fan
> Translation: I with my friend together have dinner.
>
> **我 很 喜 歡 打 藍 球** = wo hen xi huan da lan qiu
> Translation: I very like play basketball.

When words for foreign things are translated literally, the meaning can be confusing, or at the very least require some creative thinking to decipher. For example, Santa Claus in Chinese is **聖 誕 老 人** = sheng dan lao ren. When translated into English, it becomes 'Christmas old man'.

A few years ago in China, I saw a sign in a restaurant that read Roast Fire Chicken for Thanksgiving. As a Chinese speaker, I knew right away what that meant. **火 雞** (huo ji) is 'fire chicken', which means *turkey* in Chinese.

Translations from Chinese to English go really wrong when the 'translator' is too lazy to even use a good dictionary and simply uses a pocket translator or free online software, and ends up selecting some slang words.

Many people who claim to be specialists and sell their translation services to shop and restaurant owners are people who can't speak English fluently and most likely use a pocket translator themselves, which is why so many signs and menus in China are baffling and often hilarious to foreigners.

As with most countries, it is considered an asset in China to speak a second language when applying for a job. Sometimes when a company needs something translated into English, the boss may call upon one of the employees to do the task. This person probably claimed on his or her CV that he or she could speak English, but never thought it would be needed. In order to save face, the employee goes ahead with the job by browsing Google and takes the credit. The boss would have no idea what sort of a job was done. To hire a Westerner or someone with strong English translation skills is often too expensive for small Chinese companies

In many cases, Chinese companies have English signs not to appeal to English speaking customers, but to impress the non-English speaking Chinese because they think the English signs improve their image.

Another reason for widespread mistranslations is the 'cha bu duo' attitude of some of the translators. Cha bu duo (差不多) means *more or less*, *close enough* or *works anyway*. There are not usually many consequences for poor translations, because they are most likely not noticed by the Chinese people, and frequently, nobody really cares.

A few years ago in Hong Kong, I was taking a ferry to an outer island and was surprised to see the sign Go Discovery Bay instead of To Discovery Bay. The first instance is a literal translation, which is incorrect English even though it has enough of the same meaning to be clear.

Poorly translated menus can be found all over China, and they often end up being very funny and confusing. Here is an example:

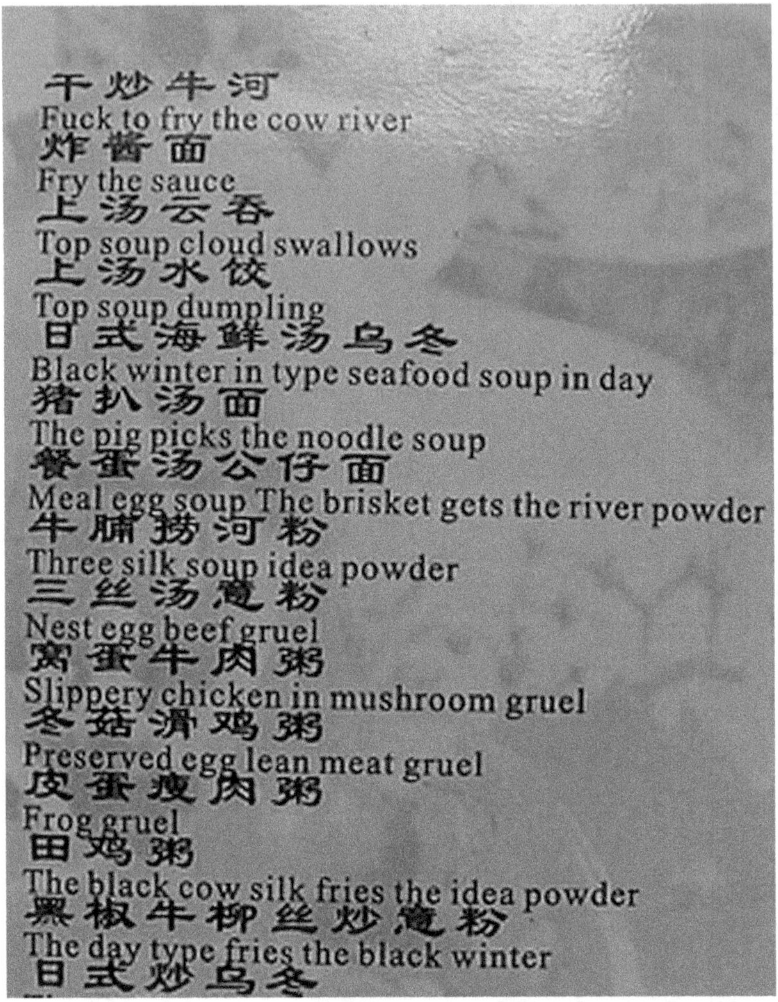

干炒牛河
Fuck to fry the cow river
炸酱面
Fry the sauce
上汤云吞
Top soup cloud swallows
上汤水饺
Top soup dumpling
日式海鲜汤乌冬
Black winter in type seafood soup in day
猪扒汤面
The pig picks the noodle soup
餐蛋汤公仔面
Meal egg soup The brisket gets the river powder
牛腩捞河粉
Three silk soup idea powder
三丝汤意粉
Nest egg beef gruel
窝蛋牛肉粥
Slippery chicken in mushroom gruel
冬菇滑鸡粥
Preserved egg lean meat gruel
皮蛋瘦肉粥
Frog gruel
田鸡粥
The black cow silk fries the idea powder
黑椒牛柳丝炒意粉
The day type fries the black winter
日式炒乌冬

This is the menu in a Cantonese restaurant, but the translation was done by a Mandarin speaker who clearly did not know any Cantonese slang or even some of the most common Cantonese dishes.

The first item is 'F*** to fry the cow river'. What on earth could that be? As a Cantonese speaker, I realized the problem right away. The dish is 'Stir fry flat rice noodle, dry' (i.e., without gravy). The first character is 'gan' which means *dry*, but it also means *f**** in Cantonese slang.

Why 'cow river'? A very popular Cantonese rice noodle is 'ngau ho', which means *cow river*. The name probably originated in an area near Cow River, not far from Canton, now Guangzhou. The Mandarin speaker who didn't know this Cantonese noodle simply directly translated the two words.

The third menu item is 'Top soup cloud swallows'. An English-speaking traveler would never know that it is simply wonton soup. Wonton in Chinese writing means *cloud swallow*. The story of how the dumping got this strange name is a long one, but you can see with a little imagination that the wontons look a bit like clouds floating in the soup broth. This dish is probably the most common Cantonese food. Most Westerners of course know it simply by the Chinese name 'wonton'; the translator complicated it unnecessarily by transcribing the literal meanings of each character.

The same idea applies to the fifth item on the menu, 'black winter.' The thick Japanese noodle is called 'Udon', which most English speakers recognize. Individually, the Chinese characters for the two syllables mean *black winter*.

The four characters in item 6—'The pig picks the noodle soup'—mean *pork chop noodle soup*. This translator's error is with the second character representing chop, which could also mean pick. Choosing the incorrect word complicates the translation.

The second to last item is 'The black cow silk fries the idea powder'. The Chinese characters literally mean 'black pepper tender beef shredding fry Italian powder' (Italian powder means *noodle*), and the dish is tender shredded beef stir fry with macaroni.

The last item, 'The day type fries the black winter', is really 'Japanese style stir fry Udon'. Japan in Mandarin is 'ri ben' (日 本), and the first character means *day*. The translator really should have known this common word, but instead only used the first character 'day' and ended up with 'the day'.

Almost every item on this menu simply makes no sense and would only confuse a hungry tourist.

Below are some really poorly translated signs.

1)

As you can see, this is not an isolated translation gone wrong. Surprisingly, these are signs from Hong Kong, which usually has excellent translations.

What they are advertising is 'salty pig trotter'. The first character means *salty* or *salted*. In Hong Kong, 'hum sup' (salty and humid) in slang means *lecherous*. A pig in Chinese also means a lecherous person, as it does in English. Pig trotter in Chinese is always referred to as 'pig's hand', because it sounds more appetizing than 'pig's feet'. But a 'salty pig's hand' refers to a lecherous groping hand, which somehow becomes 'sexual harassment' in these translations. Obviously the vendors displaying these signs have absolutely no idea what they mean.

2)

I have seen this type of sign in several provinces and over many years. The word 'crippled' is also sometimes used.

3)

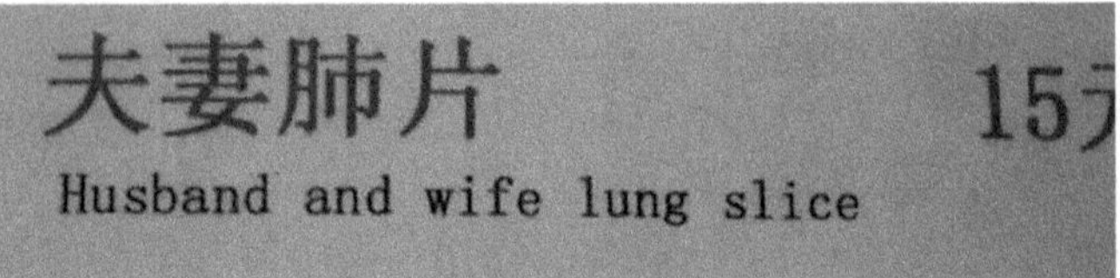

This refers to a spicy Sichuanese dish originally made with slices of lung and served cold or at room temperature. But nowadays, instead of lung, brisket and tripe are used. 'Husband and wife' are drawn in here because this dish was invented by a husband and wife team. The inexpensive dish served in their restaurant became very popular.

4)

The Chinese characters mean: One step forward (to the urinal), a big step for civilization.

5)

'No sugar food shelf' = Sugarless Food Section.

6)

7)

'Deep fry' and 'explode' share the same Chinese character. The dish is crispy deep fried large intestine.

8)

There are two kinds of bean sprouts. The ones we usually see in the US are grown from the greenish–capped mung beans. The second type grows from the yellow, larger-grained soybeans and is thicker and longer. In northern

China, they are called 'ben bean sprouts'; 'ben' means *stupid*. This dish is beef tendon and soy bean sprouts pot.

9)

10)

11)

This sign was at a busy thoroughfare in Beijing, warning drivers about the slippery road.

12)

How did this happen?

13)

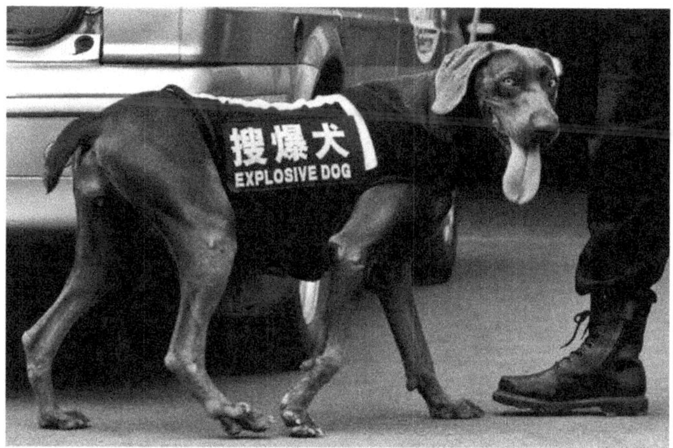

The three Chinese characters directly translated are: search explosive dog.

14)

15)

This should say: Work in progress, do not use.

16)

'From here to leave the station' in Chinese; i.e., Exit.

17)

I mentioned earlier that some companies display English writing not to attract English-speaking customers, but to impress non-English speaking Chinese customers. This is an example. It is a face cream called Grape. It claims to eliminate oiliness, but something got lost in translation once again. I certainly don't think many English-speaking customers would use it.

18)

A sign in Tibet.

19)

The 'Octopus card' in Hong Kong is a debit card for public transportation, shops, etc.

20)

There are 54 ethnic minorities in China. This is a park that showcases the various ethnic groups' costumes and cultures, etc.

21)

Third from top should be 'Colposcopy'.

22)

Your first impression of this sign might be that shoppers are mad as hell and aren't going to take it anymore! The first character means *dry*, but it is also a slang word for *f****. The five characters mean *Dry Goods Price Assessment Counter*.

23)

This sign is often seen on buffet tables in restaurants in China. The characters say, 'You should know that the food on your plate, every grain (of rice) is the result of hard work', essentially meaning *Take only what you can eat.*

24)

Seniors and children going up the ladder should be accompanied by family members.

25)

The direct translation is: 'Respect the law, care for your dog in a civilized manner'; i.e., Clean up after your dog.

26)

27)

This should be 'Pork Bowels'. The Chinese characters = Pig Internal Organs.

28)

The second character means *exercise* and is also another slang word for *f****.

29)

Cash deposit and withdrawal machine; i.e., ATM.

30)

The text along the bottom reads: 'The biggest world sports meeting will be blown up!', perhaps meaning ...*will open with a bang!*

31)

This sign could have omitted the scatological references and simply read: 'This public toilet does not need flushing. When you are finished, you can just leave.'

32)

33)

什锦牛排
Cocktail steak 128

法式鹅肝配极品牛柳 268
Need for couples with French daily

俄式怕尼尼牛扒配咸肉汁 388
Russian type afraid of someone with a whistle gravy

（套餐含：沙拉、西汤、餐包、
(Packages containing: salad, soup West, meal packages,

a) Beef with assorted vegetables.

b) 'Need for couples with French daily'? The Chinese characters mean: French style goose liver (foie gras) accompanied with tender beef.

c) 'Russian type afraid of someone with a whistle gravy' is actually a Russian style beef steak Panini with meat sauce. 'Afraid of someone' came in here because 'Pa ni ni' written in Chinese is 怕 尼 尼. The first character means *afraid*. The translator could not figure out who 'Ni Ni' was, so substituted it with 'someone'. I cannot explain the 'whistle gravy'. Some mistranslations can be rationalized; others defy logic.

34)

Mini is a popular word in China because it shares the same syllable as the verb *to entice* or *to bewitch*. In this case, it is the name of the shoe store (with 'shoe' misspelled) and not a store selling small hoes.

35)

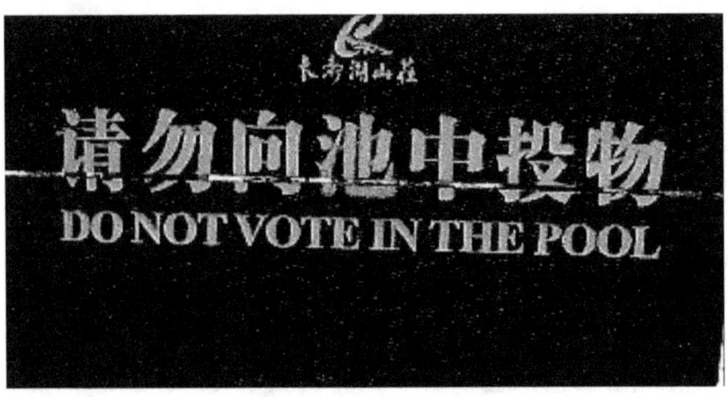

投 is the second last character, which means *to cast* or *to throw*. The character 投 is part of the word for *vote* (投票), so it's likely that the translator did a rushed or careless search. The sign means *Do not cast items into the pool.*

36)

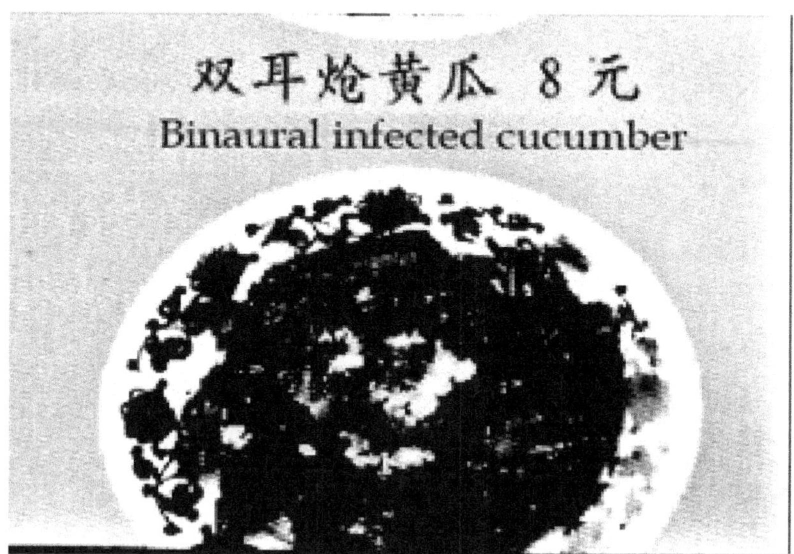

Binaural infected cucumber. Binaural means relating to or used with both ears, but I'm not sure how 'infected' got in here. It may have something to do with 'fungus', as this dish consists of two kinds of wood-ears (tree mushrooms) stir fried with cucumber.

This chapter illustrates that translation can be tricky, and sometimes downright funny. Someone who knows Chinese can especially appreciate the humor because they can often unravel how the mistranslation came about. The government is currently working to standardize many commonly used signs in China. With many young people improving their proficiency in the English language, these sorts of mistranslations will probably be seen less and less.

20

The Evolving Chinese Language on the Web

A neologism is the coining of a new word or expression, which can either be an entirely new word, or can be the adaptation of existing words to form new meanings. In modern day China, neologisms are almost entirely made up of the latter.

With around 1,600 usable syllable-tone combinations in the Chinese language, many syllables have numerous homophones that represent different meanings. In previous chapters, we have seen examples of how one syllable can represent many characters with totally different meanings. Most of the Chinese input methods for computing (described in chapter 17, Character Amnesia) are sound-based on the Pinyin method. It is easy to pick up homophones instead of the intended characters when typing into a smart phone or computer. As a result, intentional or unintentional new meanings for words appear on the Internet frequently. Some of these catch on and become established alternatives to existing words.

It is estimated that at least half of the 1.4 billion people in China are active on the popular social network Sina Weibo. One can only imagine the billions of words typed into different devices each day to be posted on this website alone. Some of the new words or new meanings of established words that appear on the web can give us a glimpse of what the Chinese language looks like in contemporary society. We can also learn a little bit about the concerns of Chinese people today from their context.

A few months ago, I was in Hong Kong reading a Chinese newspaper article about a professor in China who beat up a cleaning lady, breaking her nose, because her cart was blocking his car and he was in a hurry. The professor's barbaric behavior toward someone less privileged made international news. One of the terms used to describe this man in the article was 海 龜, which means *sea turtle*. It's a puzzling word choice from a traditional Chinese character standpoint; but 海 龜 (*sea turtle*) is the new term for 海歸 (*sea return*). Both characters have identical sounding syllables. This is a term used for Chinese (especially students) who had gone overseas and returned home.

Another hilarious new term on the web is 爱 **老虎油**(*love tiger oil*). This has nothing to do with a tiger or oil. The Chinese characters 爱 **老虎油** are pronounced aì laǒ hǔ yoú, which have similar sounds as the words 'I love you'. This term originated with the public making fun of a Chinese singer whose English was so bad that his singing of 'I love you' sounded like aì laǒ hǔ yoú!

In social networking, one of the most common neologisms is 粉 絲 (fen si), transliterated from the English word 'fans' (i.e., fans of movies or pop stars, etc.). Its meaning on the Chinese web is largely the same as that of fans in English. But the Chinese characters 粉 絲 actually mean *vermicelli*, the noodle. This is an example of how nonsensically some new terms are coined on social media. From the tenuous connection between the pronunciations of the English fans and the Chinese fen si, many other new words have sprung up, which by themselves seem absurd, but which have become commonplace on the web because their usage is so widely accepted. The characters 求粉 (qiu fen) that literally mean *beg vermicelli* now mean *beg-fans*; 互粉 (hu fen) *mutual vermicelli* means *mutual-fans*; and 回粉 (hui fen) *return vermicelli* means *return-fans*.

As Chinese society becomes more complex, many new terms have emerged for different social classes and traits. These terms are now widely used, even in daily speech:

高富帅 gao fu shuai = tall-rich-handsome, for men who are desirable.

白富美 bai fu mei = white-rich-beautiful, for women who are desirable.

窮矮搓 qiong ai cuo = poor-short-ugly, for men or women.

土肥圆 tu fei yuan = crude-fat-round, for men or women.

土豪 tu hao = local tycoon.

女神 nu shen = goddess, a charming and beautiful woman.

剩女 sheng nu = remnant-woman, a derogatory remark about women over 30 years old who are still unmarried.

There is another group of neologisms that describe specific traits or personal identity, such as:

小羅莉 xiao luo li = little Lolita, a lovely young girl aged 10 to 14.

正太 zheng tai = lovely young boy, the male counterpart of little Lolita.

偽娘 wei niang = false-woman, a man with feminine mannerism and traits.

基友 ji you = gay friend, i.e., gay man; 'ji' is transliterated from 'gay' in English.

基佬 gay lo = gay man in Cantonese. This term originated in Hong Kong.

小三 xiao san = little-three, a mistress, or a woman having an affair with a married man.

腐女 fu nu = rotten woman, a woman who likes gay men.

磚家 zhuan jia = so-called expert. This is a variant of 專家 (expert). The first character 磚 means *brick*. 'So-called experts' on the web are usually people speaking for the government instead of real experts giving honest opinions. This new word makes fun of these 'experts', essentially calling them *brick men*.

毒舌 du she = poisonous tongue, a verbally abusive person.

美眉 mei mei = pretty eyebrow, a near homophone for 妹妹 (mèi mei), which means *younger sister*. This new word keeps the meaning of younger sister but adds the extra feature that she is also beautiful.

童鞋 tong xie = child's shoe. This word now often replaces its near homophone, 同學 (tóng xué), which means *classmate* in conventional writing. 童鞋 has only come to mean *classmate* because of the similar syllables. The neologism now extends to include people from any walk of life as long as they have something in common, such as belonging to the same social club, golfers, bowlers, etc.

Political neologisms are also common on the web. In the following examples, some terms have straightforward connotations, others make little or no sense, and many come into being subversively, as a way to make political statements in a public arena that is heavily monitored by the government.

美狗 mei gou = American-dog. This refers derogatively to pro-American and pro-democracy netizens (a Western neologism made by combining Internet + citizens).

五毛 wu mao = fifty-cents. This refers to those who speak for the communist government. It derives its meaning from the alleged fifty-cent reward offered by the government for every pro-government posting made on social media.

The next two terms, 和諧 hé xíe (*harmonious*) and 河蟹 hé xìe (*river-crab*), are close homophones and recently became synonyms because the latter, *river crab*, has no political connotations and can be used without fear of censorship. The word 和諧 hé xíe (*harmonious*) may suggest questioning of the government's authority or policies, so *river crab* has come to mean the same thing among Chinese Internet users.

正腐 zhèng fŭ = currently rotting. This new word has been used as a substitute for its homophone, 政府 (zhèng fŭ), meaning *government* and containing the exact same syllables and tones. It is used derogatorily against the government, obviously insinuating that it is currently in the process of rotting. This word has been blacklisted by the Chinese government.

Another nonsensical new invention that appears in some web postings is **民煮** (min zhu), meaning *people-cook*, in place of the conventional **民住**(min zhu), meaning *democracy*. Clearly this is intentional, as the characters for *people cook* are more likely to escape notice by government monitoring than *democracy*.

中國夢 zhōng gúo mèng = China-dream. 'China-dream' is a term proposed by the leaders of the Chinese Communist Party a few years ago as a national goal, perhaps in some kind of imitation of the American Dream concept. It is idealistic and without substance, often used by the government to remind the Chinese people how good life is in China. The government propaganda machines constantly cover the bad news outside China (famines, civil war, fires, floods, and crime in the US) on TV to show the Chinese people that life outside China is tough and they should be grateful to the Chinese Communist Party. 'China-dream' has caught on as a term used sarcastically by critics of the government to refer to the extreme inequality in Chinese society, citing examples like the many elders who collect recyclable materials from garbage and resell them in order to survive.

Many other neologisms relating to everyday life have come into existence and become established thanks to the proliferation of social media and Internet posting.

One such example is 鴨梨(yā lí), now adopted by many people to mean *pressure*. The word 鴨梨 literally means *duck pear*, a type of pear grown in northern China that has a mallard-like shape, but it is a near homophone of 壓力(yā lì), which means *pressure*. It makes little sense, but 鴨梨has routinely been substituted for 壓力 and is now routinely used to mean *pressure*.

A related neologism is 鴨 梨 山 大, which is a near homophone of 亞 歷山 大, the standard Chinese translation for the English name Alexander. 山 (shan) means *mountain*; and 大 (dà) means *big*. So now it's widely understood that the name Alexander means *the pressure is as big as a mountain*.

In some cases, a new term only differs from the old one in tones, such as in 油菜花(yóu cài húa), meaning *canola flower*, as a replacement for 有才華 (yǒu cái húa) meaning *to have talents*. It's nonsensical to call someone talented a canola flower, but the term has caught on and is now used frequently.

One of the saddest new words is 失 獨 家 庭 (shī dú jīa ting), meaning *lose-only child-family*. As you might expect, it is the term for a family that has lost its only child. It's more common now because the one child policy in China has been in existence for over forty years. This is one of the worst things that can happen to a Chinese family, especially if older parents have lost their grown son or daughter and have no offspring to depend on. Most people in China do not have pensions, and social security is far too little to support them. For the family that has lost their only son, it also means the end of the family line.

This status is often viewed as a curse in China, and some believe it happens as karmic retribution for something bad someone in the family or an ancestor has done. Some families keep it a secret and suffer silently for fear that others will gloat over their misfortune.

黑心 hēi xīn (*black-heart*) is a long-standing word used all over China, originally referring to a person with bad intentions who is unscrupulous, totally without conscience, merciless, etc. In recent years, the term has been extended to mean goods and services sold by unscrupulous merchants or manufacturers, because of a series of industrial scandals in China where food products and articles for daily use were found to contain toxic materials. A number of babies died from consuming toxic milk powder in 2008. Thousands of people became ill after using 'cooking oil' that was really toxic oil recovered from industrial waste oil and recycled, processed and sold as cooking oil. Blankets stuffed with cotton salvaged from medical and industrial waste also made people ill and were called **黑心綿被**, *black-hearted quilt.*

雷 人 literally means *thunder person*, but has come to mean *stunning*. It is now colloquially used to refer to something spectacular.

There are many more neologisms in modern Chinese culture, some of which are simply too silly and esoteric to explain, and can even be difficult for a Chinese person to understand. It creates even more challenges for the foreigner trying to learn the Chinese language, but the development of new 'words' is proof that the language is alive and will continue to evolve. With the help of the Internet, a newly coined word or phrase can be seen by hundreds of million people instantaneously. The large number of homophones and the influence of the English language and Pinyin make the Chinese language particularly available for the proliferation of neologisms, making the pace of its evolution truly dizzying.

21

Japanese and the Chinese Language

It's a testament to the Chinese language that a culture as precise and efficient as Japan's has held onto the Chinese character writing system it adopted over a thousand years ago. In order to fully appreciate the Chinese writing system, one must also understand how the Japanese language works.

The origin of the spoken Japanese language is obscure. Evidence has been offered suggesting that it came from any number of sources including Ural-Altai, Polynesian and Chinese, among others. Most believe that it is connected to the Ural-Altai family, which includes the Turkic languages, Mongolian, Manchu and Korean. Prior to the introduction of the Chinese writing system, the Japanese didn't have one.

The Japanese have a complex writing system that consists of multiple systems. In addition to the thousands of Chinese characters it uses, which the Japanese call 'Kanji', meaning *Han words*, the language also utilizes two different sets of phonetic systems with about 50 syllables.

The two phonetic systems are generically called 'Kana'. Because of the complex nature of Kanji, using the Chinese characters for phonetic purposes is not feasible. The Kana systems developed independently during the 9th century as two different methods to simplify writing. Hiragana emerged as a cursive abbreviation for the Kanji and was used mostly by women, who were excluded from the study of Chinese characters. Katakana was developed by priests in Buddhist temples to use as a mnemonic device to help them read and translate Chinese works.

The result of this Chinese influence and domestic adaptation is a Japanese writing that is extremely complex with its threefold system. Part of the reason for its complexity is due to the incongruity of the Japanese and Chinese spoken languages. Every Chinese character is monosyllabic, but Japanese is a polysyllabic language. Chinese is a tonal language, whereas Japanese in not.

Hiragana and Katakana are both Kana systems, each with about 50 syllables. Each sound in the Japanese language is represented by one symbol or character (not to be confused with the Chinese character). Because these systems do not represent single consonants, they are referred to as syllabaries and not alphabets.

The use of Kana has made it possible to write a word in two ways. The Japanese word for *mountain* is a two-syllable word, 'yama', which can be written in Kana (phonetically) by using the two symbols for 'ya' and 'ma' or in Kanji by using the Chinese character 山. In Mandarin, 山 is 'shan'; but in Japanese it is 'yama'. Similarly, my family name in Chinese is 熊, meaning *bear*, and it has the sound of 'Hung' in Cantonese and 'Xiong' in Mandarin. But 熊 in Japanese is 'kuma', so the word for *bear* can be written in Kanji or in Kana using the two symbols for 'ku' and 'ma'.

Another example is 西島, meaning *west island*, which is a common Japanese name. In Chinese it is 'xi dao', but in Japanese it is 'nishijima' or 'seido', the pronunciation being dependent on the context as formal, literary or colloquial, thus adding another level of difficulty. The Japanese may write it as 西島 or as Kana using the symbols for 'ni shi' and 'ji ma'.

The Hiragana consists of five singular vowels and 43 consonant-vowel unions and is one of the basic components of the Japanese writing system. It is used to write native words for which there are no Kanji, or to write words whose Kanji form is obscure, not known to the writer or readers, or too formal for writing purposes.

The Katakana system is characterized by short, straight strokes and sharp corners, and is the simplest of the Japanese scripts. The characters are mainly used for foreign loanwords, telegrams, print advertisement, and certain onomatopoeic expressions such as 'terebi' for *television*, 'teburu' for *table*, 'biru' for *beer*, 'gurasu' for *glass*, 'aisu' for *ice*, 'takushi' for *taxi*, 'hoteru' for *hotel*, and 'sarariman' for *salary man*. This script consists of 48 symbols, with five nucleus vowels, 42 consonant-vowel unions and 1 coda consonant, the so-called 50 sounds.

As Japanese is a polysyllabic language, homophones are not as common as they are in the Chinese language. A common example of homophones in Mandarin is the syllable 'ma' which represents 媽*mother*, 麻*hemp*, 馬*horse*, 罵*to scold*, and many others. But in Japanese, all these words have two syllables, such as 馬 which is 'uma' and 麻 which is 'asa'. By being able to use the Chinese characters in multiple ways, new lexicon, ideas and vocabulary can be created, enriching the Japanese language and culture immensely.

Hiragana base characters

	a	*i*	*u*	*e*	*o*
Ø	あ	い	う	え	お
k	か	き	く	け	こ
s	さ	し	す	せ	そ
t	た	ち	つ	て	と
n	な	に	ぬ	ね	の
h	は	ひ	ふ	へ	ほ
m	ま	み	む	め	も
y	や		ゆ		よ
r	ら	り	る	れ	ろ
w	わ	ゐ		ゑ	を
	ん **(*N*)**				
Functional marks and diacritics					
つ	丶		゛	゜	

Gojūon – Katakana characters with nucleus

	a	*i*	*u*	*e*	*o*
Ø	ア	イ	ウ	エ	オ
K	カ	キ	ク	ケ	コ
S	サ	シ	ス	セ	ソ
T	タ	チ	ツ	テ	ト
N	ナ	ニ	ヌ	ネ	ノ
H	ハ	ヒ	フ	ヘ	ホ
M	マ	ミ	ム	メ	モ
Y	ヤ		ユ		ヨ
R	ラ	リ	ル	レ	ロ
W	ワ	ヰ		ヱ	ヲ

Katakana coda character

n	ン

Both Kana systems use the so-called 'fifty sound' (5x10) grid. (It is actually about 47 syllables, as 3 are no longer used.) These syllables consist of the five nucleus vowels (the top row) and 42 core syllabograms formed by combing the nine consonants with each of the five vowels. Minor differences between these two systems are beyond the scope of this book.

The word Katakana means *fragmentary Kana* and the Katakana characters are derived from components of the more complex Kanji (Chinese words).

A coda is the optional final part of a syllable, placed after its nucleus.

Why do the Japanese have two different writing systems representing the same 47 or so syllables? It's because of tradition: historically, women used Hiragana and men Katakana. When more and more foreign loanwords became incorporated into the Japanese languages, Katakana ceased to be the male-written script and became the script for non-Chinese words. This creates one more barrier to learning Japanese, especially for a Westerner who may find the Hiragana writing difficult to learn.

In addition to all this, there are two other systems: Furigana (meaning *embellishing gana*) and the Romaji (Romanization) systems.

Furigana is a Japanese reading aid made up of smaller Kana or syllabic characters printed next to a Kanji or other character to indicate its pronunciation. In modern Japan, it is mostly used in children's or learners' materials or to clarify a character. Furigana is most often written in Hiragana, although Katakana is used in certain special cases.

Once again, Romaji (Roman letters) is the application of the Latin script when writing the Japanese language. It is the Japanese equivalent of Mandarin Pinyin. It may be used in any context where Japanese text is targeted at non-Japanese speakers who cannot read Kanji or Kana, such as for names on street signs and passports.

All Japanese who have attended elementary school since WWII know how to read and write Japanese using Romaji, but it's rare in Japan to use this method to write, except as an input tool on electronic devices.

During the Meiji era (1868–1912), some Japanese scholars proposed abolishing the Kanji and even the Japanese writing systems entirely and using Romaji instead. But several attempts failed. After WWII, attempts were again made to use Romaji exclusively, and again they failed.

The Chinese character writing system has several advantages over phonetic writing systems. One reason is that the homophonous words are visually distinguishable. Another reason is that the meanings of unknown words written in Chinese characters can be surmised through the ideographic nature of these characters. The precise meaning and the configurations of these characters enable easy recognition and understanding of a passage. In addition, Chinese characters can be used to invent new words and vocabulary, just as Latin and Greek have helped to augment the English language. The Chinese characters and vocabulary are estimated to comprise no less than 50% of Japanese contemporary writing.

With such a high literacy rate in Japan, and the inherent advantages that the Chinese characters and semantics bring to the Japanese language, it's unlikely that the Chinese characters will ever be abandoned. Some scholars feel that the Japanese language, with its relatively late beginning, has become an influential world language through the clever import and smart use of the Chinese language.

In contemporary Japanese writing, all three systems are used simultaneously: the Kanji for content words, Hiragana for words such as particles and inflectional endings that indicate grammatical function, and Katakana for mainly foreign loanwords.

Below is a sample of a Japanese text, which contains all three systems of writing: Kanji, Hiragana and Katakana. Beneath the example is the transliteration (Romaji) version of the text.

Sample text in Japanese

すべての人間は、生まれながらにして自由であり、かつ、尊厳と権利とについて平等である。人間は、理性と良心とを授けられており、互いに同 胞の精神をもって行動しなければならない。

Transliteration (rōmaji)

Subete no ningen wa, umarenagara ni shite jiyū de ari, katsu, songen to kenri to ni tsuite byōdō de aru. Ningen wa, risei to ryōshin to o sazukerarete ori, tagai ni dōhō no seishinn o motte kōdō shinakereba naranai.

Translation

All human beings are born free and equal in dignity and rights. They are endowed with reason and conscience and should act towards one another in a spirit of brotherhood.
(Article 1 of the Universal Declaration of Human Rights)

You can hear a recording of the above on YouTube.

Using the Romaji system to write a non-tonal language is much more precise with less ambiguity than using the Pinyin system for the tonal Mandarin language.

Japan has always been a scientific and technologic leader. In fact, during the 1970s, the West was concerned that Japan might be taking over the world technologically. The continuing use of the Chinese character writing system didn't seem to have any deleterious effect on its science and technology.

The Japanese writing systems are difficult and not for the faint-hearted. Some students of the language are tempted to just use Romaji, which works if they simply want to communicate enough to get by. But they wouldn't be able to read or write, because nobody in Japan reads or writes in Romaji. There are very few language books in Romaji. Because the language isn't tonal, conversational Japanese is actually not that difficult to learn compared to other languages. It's the writing and reading that can drive a student mad.

Appropriating characters from the Chinese language can be a boon (for conveying new concepts, new lexicon, vocabulary, calligraphy as an art form), and a bane (difficult ideograms, memory intensive). Japanese personal and place names are written nearly all in Chinese characters. A number of these were created in Japan and are only understood there, and although none of them can be found in a Chinese dictionary, they look very much like Chinese characters. It's likely that the utility of the Chinese language will continue to override its complications, and will endure as an integral part of the Japanese language.

22

Korean and the Chinese Language

Various theories have been proposed to explain the origin of the Korean language. The most widely accepted one is that, like Japanese, it belongs to the Altaic family.

Chinese writing has been known in Korea for over 2,000 years. The Koreans have borrowed nearly 70% of their vocabulary from the Chinese language, giving many of the Chinese characters (which they call Hanja) Korean readings and/or meanings. They also invented about 150 new characters, most of which are rare and are mainly for personal use or represent place names, just as Japan has done.

Hangul (also spelled Hangeul), the Korean alphabet, was invented in 1444. It consists of only 24 characters, 14 of which are consonants and 10 of which are vowels. Combinations of these letters represent 5 double consonants and 11 diphthongs. An example of the Hangul alphabet is shown here:

ㄱ g, ㄴ n, ㄷ d, ㄹ l/r, ㅁ m, ㅂ b, ㅅ s, ㅇ null

The letters, put together in clusters of two, three or four, form syllable blocks or boxes. Note that there is a phenomenon in the Korean alphabet of using 'ㅇ' or null. How this letter is used is beyond the scope of this book.

The invention of Hangul is a great achievement in the history of Korean culture because it has contributed to one of the highest literary rates in the world.

The formation of words using Hangul is very different from the way Western alphabets are used to form words. The emphasis is on the formation of a syllable block with the end result bearing some resemblance to a Chinese character. The components can be stacked up on top of one another, or placed sideways, unlike other alphabets that always place letters in a linear manner. The whole syllabic grouping forms a syllabic 'box' or 'block', and these are strung together to form words.

Traditionally, like Chinese, Korean was written from right to left in vertical columns; today, the majority of texts are written from left to right in horizontal lines.

The Hangeul alphabet (한글)

ㄱ	ㄲ	ㄴ	ㄷ	ㄸ	ㄹ	ㅁ
기역 giyeok	쌍 기역 ssang giyeok	니은 niən	디귿 digət	쌍 디귿 ssang digət	리을 riəl	미음 miəm
g, k	kk	n	d, t	tt	l	m
k, g	kk	n	t, d	tt	l, r	m
[k/g]	[k*]	[n]	[t/d]	[t*]	[l/r]	[m]

ㅂ	ㅃ	ㅅ	ㅆ	ㅇ	ㅈ	ㅉ
비읍 biəp	쌍 비읍 ssang biəp	시옷 shiot	쌍 시옷 ssang shiot	이응 iəng	지읒 jiət	쌍 지읒 ssang jiət
b, p	pp	s	ss	ng	j	jj
p, b	pp	s	ss	-ng	ch, j	tch
[p/b]	[p*]	[s]	[s*]	[Ø/-ŋ]	[ʧ/ʤ]	[ʧ*]

ㅊ	ㅋ	ㅌ	ㅍ	ㅎ
치읓 chiət	키읔 kiuek	티읕 tiət	피읖 piəp	히읗 hiət
ch	k	t	p	h
ch’	k’	t’	p’	h
[ʧ^{h}]	[k^{h}]	[t^{h}]	[p^{h}]	[h]

The table above contains 14 consonants plus 5 double consonants.

The next table contains 10 vowels plus 11 diphthongs (combining two vowels in a single syllable).

ㅏ	ㅐ	ㅑ	ㅒ	ㅓ	ㅔ	ㅕ	ㅖ
a	ae	ya	yae	eo	e	yeo	ye
a	ae	ya	yae	ŏ	e	yŏ	ye
[a]	[æ]	[ja]	[jæ]	[ʌ]	[e]	[jʌ]	[je]
ㅗ	ㅘ	ㅙ	ㅚ	ㅛ	ㅜ	ㅝ	ㅞ
o	wa	wae	oe	yo	u	wo	we
o	wa	wae	oe	yo	u	wŏ	we
[o]	[wa]	[wæ]	[we]	[jo]	[u]	[wʌ]	[we]
ㅟ	ㅠ	ㅡ	ㅢ	ㅣ			
wi	yu	eu	ui	i			
wi	yu	ŭ	ŭi	i			
[wi]	[ju]	[ɨ]	[ɨj]	[i]			

How to spell in Hangul

The syllables or sounds for the two large Chinese characters are 'han' and 'ja' meaning *Han word*. Below the Chinese characters is the spelling in Hangul for *Hanja*.

'Han' is composed of 3 symbols just like in English: h, a, n. The 'h' is on the left top, 'the 'a' is on the right top, and 'n' is at the bottom.

'Ja' is composed of 2 symbols, 'j' and 'a'. The 'j' is on the left and the 'a' is on the right.

Writing Korean is a matter of learning the alphabet and learning how to place the different symbols (characters) to form syllables. Putting syllables together will then produce words. The syllable 'han' in Hangul can mean more than one thing, whereas the Chinese character 漢is very specific. The biggest advantage that the Chinese character writing system has over phonetic writing systems is that the precise meaning and the configuration of these characters enable easy recognition and understanding of a passage.

In the Korean alphabet, g and k share one phoneme; b and p also share one phoneme; and l and r share one as well. This explains why the character 李, a common family name in Korea, can be pronounced as 'Li' or 'Rhee'.

Like other languages, Korean has to deal with homophones. For example, in Korean, the words for the following all have the same two syllables of 'sey oo': *spiritual discipline*, *prisoner*, *Venice* (or *city of water*), *paddy rice*, *drain*, *tunnel* and *capital* (city). If they are written in Hangul, the reader must take the context into consideration to find the right word. But in Hanja (Chinese characters), there is no ambiguity, as each word contains completely different characters with specific meanings. Another example of a Korean homophone is the syllable 'bae', which can mean *stomach*, *pear* or *a ship floating on the sea.*

In areas like medicine, history, business or law, Hangul may not be adequate, and Hanja may be needed to clarify certain parts of the text.

On the next page are examples of a text in Hangul only and another that is a hybrid of Hangul and Hanja. The Hanja, though more difficult to write, is more precise in meaning, making the passage easier to understand.

Sample text in Korean (hangeul only)

모든 인간은 태어날 때부터 자유로우며 그 존엄과
권리에 있어 동등하다. 인간은 천부적으로 이성과 양심을
부여받았으며 서로 형제애의 정신으로 행동하여야 한다.

Sample text in Korean (hangeul and hanja)

모든 人間은 태어날 때부터 自由로우며 그 尊嚴과
權利에 있어 同等하다. 人間은 天賦的으로 理性과 良心을
賦與받았으며 서로 兄弟愛의 精神으로 行動하여야 한다.

Transliteration

Modeun Ingan-eun Tae-eonal ttaebuteo Jayuroumeyeo Geu Jon-eomgwa Gwonrie Iss-eo Dongdeunghada. Ingan-eun Cheonbujeog-eruo Iseong-gwa Yangsim-eul Bu-yeobad-ass-eumyeo Seoro Hyungje-ae-ui Jeongsin-euro Haengdongha-yeo-yahanda.

(The meaning of this text, about Human Rights, is the same as the one used for the Japanese example in the previous chapter.)

Like the Japanese, the Koreans also have a love-hate relationship with the Chinese characters. They can be useful and specific, making communication more clear; but it also takes a long time to learn the characters. South Korea actually stopped teaching Hanja to its students for a time, and then reversed the policy. Government policy-makers concluded that they couldn't do away with the Chinese characters entirely because of the many homophonic words they had adopted from the Chinese. Now, about 2,000 commonly used Hanja letters are taught in South Korean secondary schools.

For a language containing 70% Chinese words, which cannot avoid homonyms, solely using a phonetic system may not be adequate. A survey of South Koreans showed that 89% of them support Hanja education. After banning Hanja-Hangul mixed script for decades, South Korea is bringing it back, using Chinese characters for words of Chinese origin and Hangul for Korean words.

The government has tried to push Romanization of the Korean language, but it's been met with great resistance from the people and hasn't caught on. The temptation to use the Latin alphabet is great, since most people in the world already know it; but it would be a tremendous effort for someone to learn a new alphabet. The barrier of learning a new language may be too high.

Another reason that Romanization of the Korean language hasn't occurred is that the Hangul alphabet is Korean in origin and is thought to be one of the most intelligently designed and phonetically consistent systems in the world, and is a source of great pride for the Korean people.

In addition, abandoning the Chinese-inspired box-like beauty of Hangul might be aesthetically undesirable: that box is seemingly an integral part of expressing the soul and imaginings for Korean calligraphers.

When I worked with the Uyghur people in Xinjiang off and on for ten years, I really wanted to learn their language, which is very similar to Turkish. I had no problem learning Turkish, which uses a modified Latin alphabet; but unfortunately, the Uyghur language had just switched from using the Latin alphabet to the Arabic alphabet. I simply didn't have the time to learn the Arabic alphabet.

Korea, like Japan, continues to use Chinese characters even after some serious efforts to do without them. Perhaps the

Chinese can learn from the Japanese and Koreans, and develop a hybrid system using the Chinese characters for names and specific terms, and Pinyin for common things. The world is changing so rapidly; who knows what kind of writing system China will end up with?

Conclusion

These are changing times as IT continues to move forward at an incredible speed. I don't think anybody knows how the Chinese written language will look in twenty years, but in my opinion, it seems likely that fewer and fewer people will be able to recall from memory how to write many of the Chinese characters. The consolation is that recognizing the characters is much easier than having to actually write them out. With developing technologies, Chinese speakers can communicate over the Internet without much difficulty by using the Pinyin or voice recognition input systems. They must simply be able to recognize the characters so they can choose the correct ones shown on the screen.

The opinion of most language scholars is that the simplification of the characters hasn't saved the people that much time. It's unclear how much it has helped to improve literacy. In 2013, the Chinese Ministry of Education announced that there are now 8,000 standard characters with 2,501 of them having been simplified. Most dictionaries list less than 20,000 characters, even though there are over 50,000. An educated Chinese person will know about 8,000.

The simplification of these characters seems to have caused more problems than it has solved. Some even suggest that, paradoxically, it is actually more difficult to remember the simplified characters as they don't follow any pattern, may not contain familiar radicals, have no history and have little reference to other characters. In fact, there is a movement in China to revert the simplified characters back to the original script. People who have learnt the simplified form find it very difficult to, or simply cannot, read books printed before the language reform.

From my own experience, having been educated in the traditional script, it's a slow process to read a newspaper containing simplified characters; and sometimes I can't figure out the characters no matter how hard I try to guess. I recently watched an old Hong Kong movie with my favorite actress in it, whose surname is 葉, which means *leaf*. But in the YouTube title, her name was given as 叶 in the simplified form. How could 葉 become 叶? It makes sense for the character 葉 to represent *leaf* because the radical on the top means *vegetation*. What made the language reformers decide to use 叶 to represent *leaf*? Rather than a simplification of the original, it seems to be an entirely new character. It takes almost as long to write 叶 as it does 葉.

It's plausible that eventually the Chinese will adopt a hybrid writing system, using the Pinyin for common everyday language, while keeping the Chinese characters for more specific terms and names as the Japanese and Korean have done.

A hybrid system could make writing Chinese easier than its current form. I'll use the Universal Declaration of Human Rights once again to demonstrate how a hybrid system might be used.

In traditional characters:

人人生而自由，在尊嚴和權利上一律平等。他們附有理性和良心，並應以兄弟關係的精神互相對待。

In a hybrid system:
Renren sheng er ziyou, zai zunyan 尊嚴 he quanli 權利 shang yilu pingden. Tamen fuyou lixing 理性 he liangxin 良心, bing yingyi xiongdi guanxi de jingshen 精神 huxiang duidai.

Translation:
All human beings are born free and equal in dignity and rights. They are endowed with reason and conscience and should act towards one another in a spirit of brotherhood.

Using the characters to clarify terms such as *dignity*, *rights*, *reason* and *conscience* eliminates any ambiguity or misunderstanding that can result from the language's many homonyms, which appear the same in Pinyin but different in Chinese characters. Perhaps it would be a flexible system in which the writer decides how much Pinyin to use, or the number of characters required to clarify his or her writing in order to avoid confusion.

As far as classical Chinese and literature in traditional writings are concerned, they would likely be left to scholars who specialize in such areas. That way, nothing would be lost, and the Chinese would keep their culture and their language intact. Most of them would likely still be able to appreciate or even write poems in the traditional Chinese script. For those who were interested and willing to spend the time, they could bring themselves to any level of proficiency, learning far more than the 2,000 characters required for literacy.

The hybrid system of writing is far from the perfect solution, as it still requires learning the 2,000 or so characters. Mostly likely, as people get more and more used to using Pinyin, fewer and fewer characters will be needed for clarification.

During the last twenty years or so, IT has permeated almost every aspect of our lives. The Chinese language has evolved along with it. People simply do what is the easiest, most convenient and workable for them. The evolution of Chinese writing will eventually be decided by the people who use it. Languages are alive; they all evolve.

Whatever the future of the Chinese language, it would be a shame if the Chinese script, with all its history, beauty and complexity, were to completely disappear.

About the Author

James Y. Hung grew up in Hong Kong and Malaysia. He was educated in both the English and Chinese languages at an early age. He did his undergraduate studies in liberal arts at the University of Hawaii and obtained his MD degree from the University of Nebraska.

After retirement from his private practice in retinal surgery, Dr. Hung has renewed his interest in the Chinese language and Tang poetry, which he finds fascinating. He has published peered reviewed articles on retinal surgery as well as several books of general interest and an ophthalmology book for non-ophthalmologists.

He now mainly lives in Honolulu, Hawaii and continues his volunteer work in different parts of the world.

www.ingramcontent.com/pod-product-compliance
Lightning Source LLC
LaVergne TN
LVHW051504080426
835509LV00017B/1904
* 9 7 8 0 6 9 2 9 2 4 9 5 2 *